MW00761642

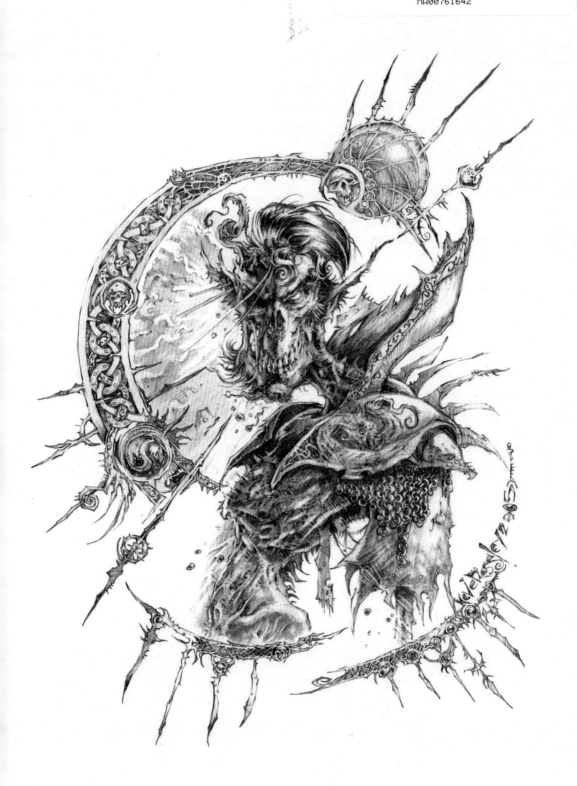

Dedicated to Steve Morger. More than the best of friends.
Liam Sharp

CONTRIBUTORS

Douglas Rushkoff
Steve Niles
Liam Sharp
Dan Wickline
Kody Chamberlain
Brian Holguin
Dave Kendall
Ali Powers
Emma Simcock-Tooth
Ash Wood
Kev Crossley
Rich Johnston
Saverio Tenuta
Shane McCarthy
Cardinal
Samuel Araya
Chris Weston
Gary Erskine
Ralph R. Raims
Bagwell
John Bamber
John Howard
Lee Carter
Tom Muller
Roger M. Cormack
Brem
Karl Spracklen
Steven Perkins
Glenn Fabry

MAM TOR™ would also like to thank:

Mike Lake
Dez Skinn
Roger and Linda Sharp
Kerry Ford
Enrico Salvini
Kevin Eastman
Beau Smith
Gary Lawford
Kevin Crossley
Dave Kendall

MAM TOR EVENT HORIZON™

21st Century Pulp Fiction

BOOK 1 OF 12, Published by MAM TOR™ PUBLISHING LTD.

MAM TOR Publishing™

EDITOR-IN-CHIEF	LIAM SHARP
EDITORIAL ASSISTANT	DAWN FINCHAM
DESIGN	TOM MULLER
PRODUCTION	CHRISTINA MC_CORMACK
SUBMISSIONS EDITORS	JOHN BAMBER / JASON HARRIS
BUSINESS DEVELOPMENT	JOHN MC_PHERSON

HTTP://WWW.MAMTOR.COM   INFO@MAMTOR.COM

VISIT THE OFFICIAL MAM TOR™ PUBLISING WEBSITE FOR ALL THE LATEST
NEWS. ART PREVIEWS. DOWNLOADS. AND CREATOR INFORMATION.

ISBN: 0-9549998-0-0

Mam Tor: EVENT HORIZON™ Book 1 of 12. May 2005. FIRST PRINTING.
MAM TOR™ PUBLISHING. PO BOX 6785 / Derby DE22 1XT / United Kingdom.
Mam Tor: EVENT HORIZON™ is TM & © Copyright MAM TOR™ PUBLISHING LTD. All contents copyright the respective credited creators. All rights reserved
With the exception of artwork used for review purposes none of the contents of this publication may be reproduced without the prior permission of
MAM TOR™ PUBLISHING. The stories, characters and incidents depicted in this publication are entirely fictional.

Printed in the USA

Preface by Douglas Rushkoff

● WWW.RUSHKOFF.COM

We underestimate a medium at our own peril.

WE UNDERESTIMATE A MEDIUM AT OUR OWN PERIL.

Particularly one as unassuming and kid-friendly as comics.

But comics have a way of surprising you - like that second hit of acid you take just before you realize the first one is actually coming on a lot stronger than you expected. Once you're into the trip that far, and committed for more, all that's left to do is hang on and push through.

This stuff works in the gutters - the spaces between the panels, and between the pictures and words. Unlike a movie, which comes at you in one smooth stream of light and sound, or a book, which takes you on a linear journey, words flowing off the page like toothpaste out of the tube, comic art works on more than one level and at more than one time.

More like an incantation than a narrative, a kaleidoscope than a point of view, a sequence of images than portrait of anything, the succession of words and pictures on the following pages combine to create a mosaic that you must put together, yourself. No post-modernism needed, here; the world ahead is pre-deconstructed.

And as you put all this together in your head (if that's where your thinking happens to take place) youill realize that this alchemical process is unique for its ability to convey the spaces between things. The liminal zones between waking and sleeping, alive and dead, or reality and fantasy.

This is where Mam Tor's writers and artists spend their time, and their work invites you to pass over the lip of the event horizon and closer to the strange attractor from which these bizarre visions surely emanate.

Yeah, it's monsters, weird dreams, alternate realities, and forgotten worlds, but rendered in ways that promise to sneak past a reader's literary defenses and a moviegoer's jaded cynicism. By hitting you with images both primal and fantastic, and language both vernacular and magickal, these pages have the potential to open up a liminal space in your own cognitive matrix.

And though you may close this book when youire done, that space may take much longer to heal over.

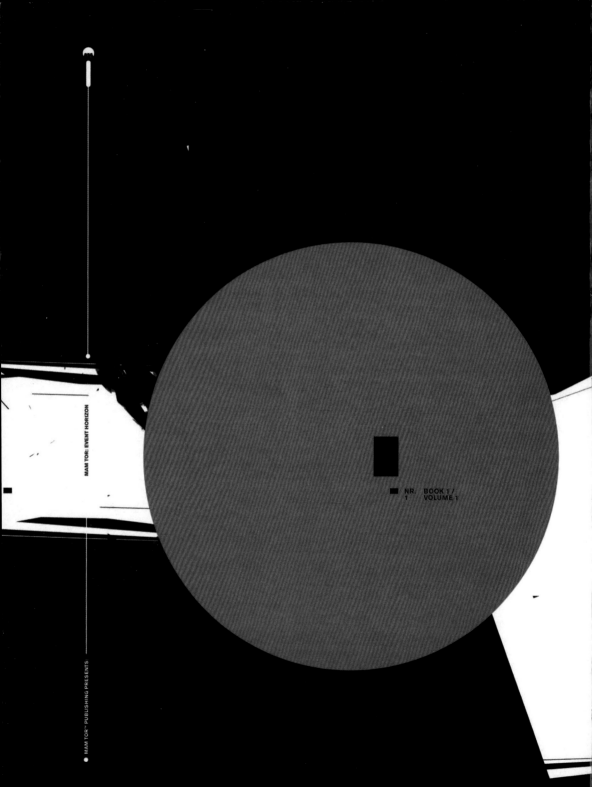

MAM TOR: EVENT HORIZON

● MAM TOR™ PUBLISHING PRESENTS

NR.   BOOK 1 /
1   VOLUME 1

CONTENTS

PIN-UP GALLERY

MAM
TOR
Publishing

Steve Niles • Liam Sharp

fucking savages

There are ages, my children, that few can remember.
Dark cities once sprawled across young lands, saprophytic and vast.
And men - then as now - sought answers and power.
Kingdoms were born and kingdoms died.
Empires reached their zenith, mastered the world,
before disappearing into the dark recesses of time, forgotten.
And yet more ancient races still walked shadowy paths across war-torn continents,
seeking peace, final oblivion, or an impossible return to their former glories.

This was no easy age for men! But then, whenever was there such a time?

Hellicarnum and *Malthaxus* were the great cities of the east,
thriving on thuggery and fear.
Their dominion spread over a thousand miles,
beyond the Maw of Surmum
and deep into the bleak wilderness of Ghethé.
It was wary respect alone that kept the two powers so long intact.

And unto this age a new legend was born.
One that would outlast even the cities themselves,
and the evils that spawned them.

In time there would be raised a small fellowship
the likes of which the world had never before seen!
Their deeds, good and bad,
would inform whole generations as yet unborn.
They were the prototype,
forged in primeval chaos and agony,
for the hero-army.

The *super-team*.

Their passage would one day instill awe - and dread!

But, as with so many great tales,
it all started with just one man...

I have seen ten thousand men die on a single day, on one battlefield.
I have witnessed women and children choking on their own entrails.
I have seen the worst the world has to offer, and still, I am here.
It is a lesson my enemies learn often.

You can show me your worst, but I will always come back.

So next time you fuck with me, make sure I am dead.

Aye; and I left more than my sword in yer woman, Savage! What do ya think of that?

Care to sample the stew, good sir?

Smells good.

Like **VICTORY**, aye Savage?

No sad and weepy tale from me you'll hear. That I promise. I simply lay the facts out as I see them.

It was my error to allow myself to settle with that woman, to allow myself the luxury of comfort. I allowed myself to fall in love.

And by falling in love I handed myself over to her family and in turn the village.

I allowed myself comfort, and when the pigs came hunting I handed Lord Borbos my weakness on a golden platter... my heart.

And now I will take it back and introduce them to theirs and so much more.

Look! The king of the barbarians brings us soup!

Ha-ha-ha-ha-ha-ha
Ha-ha-ha-ha-ha-ha-ha

Ha-ha-ha-ha-ha-ha-ha

Guards! Hold him!

It is my people's **tradition** to offer a stew made of our best livestock and harvest beans as a symbol of our **SURRENDER** to mighty warriors. You, Lord Borbos invaded and conquered us.

It is your **right**.

You must think me a **fool**.

I will sample after everyone has had a taste...
There, that's it!

It took not long for the Pig King to have the pot himself

Sit with us and drink and we will discuss the defeat of your village and the role it will play, if any, in the future of my city.

The bellies of his thugs were full and he knew there was no poison in the mix.

I admire a man who knows when he is **defeated**.
I will make you **king of the slaves** if you so wish.

What of my people, those you did not defeat?

They will be used for some purpose I suppose.
The women are only good for a while... then they will be hung.
The men will work the fields and the children as well.

My people have lived here for as long as they've known.
We have many talents as the delicious stew suggests.
Why resort to labor and violation?

Talents?

See this length of ordinary Bamboo from the islands?

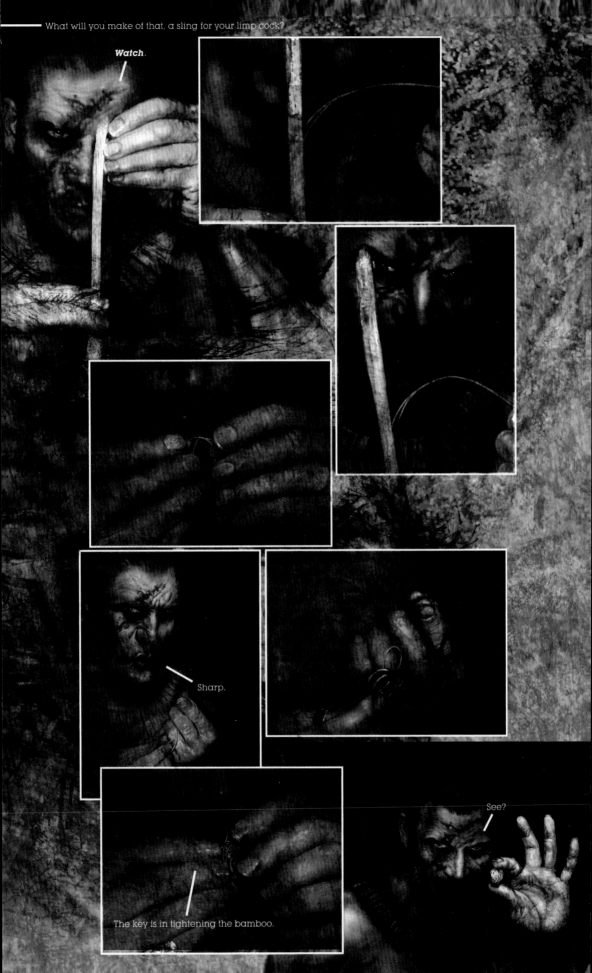

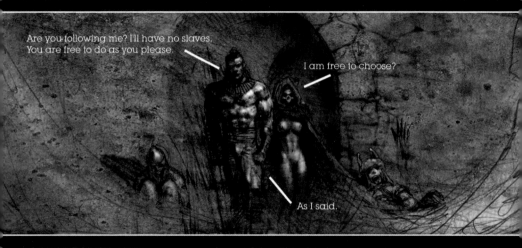

Are you following me? I'll have no slaves. You are free to do as you please.

I am free to choose?

As I said.

Then I choose to be with you, if you'll have me.

There it is then.

How easily I fall into the trap of companionship again. I take the bait like starving fish.

It is the cycle and tragedy of my kind and my time. Should I deny future pain by ignoring possible pleasure?

I will take it, and if taken again, blood will be spilled... again.

Where will we go?

I will know... when we are there.

IT WAS AN AGE OF WAR AND CRUSADES.

AN AGE WHERE A MAN PICKED UP A SWORD LONG BEFORE HE EVER LAID DOWN WITH A WOMAN..

HE WOULD TAKE A LIFE BEFORE LEARNING HOW TO LIVE ONE.

LORNE HAD KILLED MANY TIMES IN THE NAME OF HIS KING.

HE TASTED HIS SHARE OF BLOOD AND HAD REACHED HIS FILL.

UPON HIS LAST RETURN FROM THE WEST, HE BESEECHED HIS KING FOR A WAY HE COULD CONTINUE TO SERVE WITHOUT THE BLOODSHED.

THE KING KNEW LORNE'S DEVOTION TO THE CROWN AND THAT THE REQUEST WAS NOT MADE LIGHTLY.

THE KING MADE LORNE THE KEEPER OF THE ROYAL HERD.

HIS JOB WAS SIMPLE.

SERFS WOULD FEED AND CARE FOR THE ANIMALS.

HIS ONLY CONCERN WAS THE SAFETY OF THE HERD.

STORY DAN WICKLINE • ART KODY CHAMBERLAIN

VANISHING
HERD

A FORTNIGHT AGO THE HERD'S NUMBERS BEGAN TO DWINDLE. IT WOULD NOT BE ODD FOR AN OCCASIONAL STRAY; BUT SIX IN AS MANY DAYS WAS A SIGN OF DANGER.

SOMETHING WAS HUNTING THE HERD AND IT WAS TIME FOR LORNE TO DO SOME HUNTING OF HIS OWN.

HE WOULD TRAVEL LIGHT. NO NOISY ARMOR TO SLOW HIM DOWN OR ANNOUNCE HIS PRESENCE.

HOURS PASSED WITH NOT SO MUCH AS A SQUIRREL CROSSING HIS PATH.

UNTIL SUDDENLY...

HE WOULD HUNT AT NIGHT FOR THAT WAS WHEN HIS PREY WAS OUT.

LORNE WAS CERTAIN HE HAD FOUND HIS PREY.

A WOLF SO CLOSE TO THE HERD WAS DANGEROUS ENOUGH.

BUT THE REMAINS OF HIS KILLS LYING ABOUT THE GROUND MADE IT ALL TOO CLEAR.

LORNE HAD DRAWN SWORDS ON THE FIELD OF BATTLE MORE TIMES THAN HE CAN REMEMBER, BUT HE KNEW THE MEN HE FACED UNDERSTOOD WHY.

THE THOUGHT OF KILLING AN ANIMAL FOR MERELY FOLLOWING ITS NATURE MADE HIM SICK.

BUT HE HAD SWORN TO PROTECT THE HEARD.

ONCE MORE FOR THE KING.

HIS ATTEMPT TO AVOID KILLING HAD FAILED.

HE WOULD TAKE THE WOLF BACK AND BURY IT PROPERLY.

THE SILENCE OF THE NIGHT WAS ONCE AGAIN INTERRUPTED...

BUT THIS TIME IT WAS THE SOUND OF HORSES THAT CAUGHT LORNE'S ATTENTION.

LORNE HAD JUST REGAINED HIS TASTE FOR KILLING...

WITH A *VENGEANCE.*

The Gallows God

Writer Brian Holguin
Artist Dave Kendall

MACHIVARIUS
POINT:
AVATAR

A sequence by Roger M. Cormack

Prelude:

> "There was once a cold and empty place. Lonely civilisations lived beneath blind stars. Stranded sailors died on desolate rocks, their ships splintered upon the hostile shores of faraway lands.

> "The Weeping God loved Its children, despairing that they did not know one another, living alone as they did in such emptiness. So it spun for them a great web, casting it out over the stars, so that It's children would never again know loneliness.

> "And we, the children, have walked those gossamer trails that bind the stars, and we are not afraid, for we know we are not alone. And we know we are loved.
> The Weeping God has forged for us a way home. A bridge through the darkness.
> Sailors need never die alone on cruel shores again.
> He has bound us all in the infinite web that they who know of it have come to call:

> "KIAZMUS!"

> Anon. 1700BC.

I

Brec, lashed to an empty wine barrel, watched as ragged golden sails pitched, dipped out of view once more, and were finally gone.

The chill sea was brutal. He hated the wet. One long campaign had taken him across the endless peat bogs of Kos Moor and Dunn Fell, themselves rutted like an earthen ocean. The perpetual rainfall had driven the gnarly mercenary near to madness, but the sea revealed a new truth: It's waters were a far harsher element than rain could ever be.

He felt he should be at home upon the sea - in some obscure way it reached out to him. Yet it engendered a troubling sense of loss he could not comprehend - and so he gave it only his hatred.

The night was spent in churning isolated darkness. Distant calls from other survivors occasionally punctuated the monotony. But in time they waned, and eventually ceased altogether.

Now the sun bobbed at the zenith of it's low winter arc, suggesting warmth, but offering up none. The abrasive hemp lashing of his makeshift raft chaffed the flesh of his swollen white fingers. His body dangled all but obsolete beneath the waves. Eventually their moronic rhythm - peak after trough after peak - lulled Brec into a stupor. His mind lurched, drunk on fractured memories of what now seemed better days...

A tribe of Mercenaries calling themselves the Umbriani chanced upon Brec's childhood home. Breeden village, sprawling chaotically along side the river Florth at the foot of Wealdenhead Tor, had been a yolk to the boy. It was all he had ever known in that distant, less violent past. Methuselah Kush, the wolf-shanked mercenary Chieftain, noticed Brec's uncommon bulk, the steady ice-cool gaze of his green eyes. He compelled the youth to undertake a variety of labours, which Brec completed with an easy - if somewhat belligerent - facility. That night a bargain was compacted with his parents. Wine was consumed. Tears shed.

The following morning sunlight struck the summit of Wealdenhead Tor, bathing it in flame. The Umbriani were back on the march, their numbers swollen by one.

Brec, clinging to his makeshift raft, could not recall having thought about his parents for a moment beyond that day.

Gingerly he opened salt-stung eyes, blinking against the light.

Nothing.

No lonely jutting spur of rock, no distant loom of an island. Not even the fluting caw of a gull.

The cold seemed to burn him now, engulfing him in waves of feverish heat. Soon his mind was back, adrift in other memories.

Back in the Suusa Desert. Back in that breath robbing swelter.

Back in the Patthylyon campaign, fighting for his life.

Cut off from the bulk of the Umbriani, he had bulwarked himself and his men in a tight fissure of scorched earth. For five fraught days he had managed to keep the ebony onslaught of the Maasoom at bay. The red-eyed tribesmen could not penetrate his stronghold. But neither could he escape it.

Somehow a craggy wall was erected, rough steps hewn, and on the sixth day he broke free of the defile and rejoined the mercenaries, swinging the odds in their favor.

They feasted that evening. Triple rations gorged as the heads of a hundred braves gazed blindly down from their staves.

Brec could no longer distinguish day from night.

Vaguely he hoped a shark or some other oceanic predator might take him, honor him with one last battle. The kind of heroic ideal for death he had been raised to approve of.

It would have been an ill-made match.

The thuggish slap, the monotonous swell and retreat of waves, continued to lull and confuse his senses. The inescapable cold suggested another coldness to him, awakening a memory in which he shuddered, half buried under dank, snow-beaten bracken.

His beloved Umbriani had been decimated. Brec and a handful of others - all that remained of over three hundred men - had escaped into the vast and largely uncharted primordial gloom of the Tollos Forrest.

A bear had found him in his hiding place. It had reared, startled, falling on him like a landslide.

It took him months to recover - he yet bore livid scars - but he crafted a fine cloak out of that bear's hide, and for many years it contributed greatly to his legend.

(He imagined the bedraggled thing now, spiraling down into unknowable depths. A belated resting-place. The waterlogged skin had threatened to drag him with it, but he had managed to cut it free.

No other man would claim it as a trophy at least, and he contented himself with that.)

An age later, he half smiled to recall, had seen his reputation grow and precede him. He had become a lone mercenary, sometime bodyguard, and, if work was scarce, assassin. He balked at the memory of this last. Brec much preferred his open notoriety, the fearful appraisals his bearskin mantle attracted, to the darker deeds of a fugitive assassin.

Such nakedly animalistic men often (perplexingly, and predictably,) attract women of charm, even high birth. In near global travels Brec seldom looked far for a soft bed, a willing fuck. His large cock (whilst not the legend it was proported to be) and surprising tenderness perpetuated an entirely different fame.

However, such trysts were ultimately little more than sport, or relief. He felt little for the women who writhed in his surly embrace, vainly hoping to add his name to their own, his legend to their meager histories. There was a gap within him - he knew it, but not why - and though he couldn't remember it, he knew the gap had a name.

Darkness subsided, giving way to a throbbing golden-red beyond his eyelids.
Brec - his half open mouth suddenly invaded by swirling tumultuous brine - groped his way urgently toward wakefulness.

Supporting himself upon a shaky elbow, Brec hauled in a long, shuddering breath, then puked violently in the shallow seawater lapping about him. His numb fingers curled in the sand.
Land!
He cut himself free of the barrel and made his way up the beach on unsteady legs that felt like they did not belong to him. The sky was cloudless, the air warm, with only the faintest bite to suggest winter. He was, he supposed, on one of the many volcanic islands that huddled conspiratorially a days sailing west of Corthallia. The nearest land beyond that was Hulffennland, where they had been bound, almost a month's journey northward. He would build a raft - there was plenty of vine and wood - and head back to the Isthmus of Corthallia. It should take no more than three days, he calculated.
By that evening he had located a source of fresh water and butchered a fat Plattofowl he found wandering through the scrub. He started a small fire and was soon dining on the tough, rich meat of the flightless bird. The stars glittered above the now tranquil mirror of the sea, and the greasy carcass of the Plattofowl filled the air with its oily sweet scent. Brec was glad of his life. He was a solitary being. A soldier. He had been through a lot worse.
The following morning he awoke feeling much more akin to his usual self. It was only in sitting up that he realised how wrong that perception was.
Where once the sea swelled lazily there now stretched an ocean of ochre sand. Behind him the landscape had also been inexplicably altered. The lush verdant undergrowth and giant palms of the previous day had been transplanted with a wall more impressive in its sheer scale than anything he had seen in his life. Worst of all, to his mind at least, he found himself naked. Weapon-less.
Brec had always been a decisive man, capable of making the most of unusual, or unexpected situations. Unable to comprehend his disconcerting circumstances, he chose to momentarily accept them. At length he began to walk alongside the featureless wall in the cool of its ominous shadow. Either he had, he reasoned, stumbled there delirious in the night. Or he still bobbed, close to death, strapped to a barrel in the open sea.
The day wore on. Soon a too-high and exacting sun beat unmercifully down upon his broad umber shoulders. He could take that. His skin had almost turned to leather over many years of stoic, often self-induced hardship. Nevertheless, by midday the magnitude of his situation was setting in, as there had been no window, door, or opening of any kind within the inscrutable expanse of the wall. Bitterly he supposed that, had he in fact stumbled there in the night, then he must have come from the other direction - a half-day's walk had not returned him to the sea after all. At best, he could hope to be back at the sea's edge by nightfall. At worst, the dawn should see him there. With this in mind, and armed with his usual dogged resolve, Brec turned around and retraced his route with scarcely a break in pace.

There had been wonders in his life, Brec thought, as he followed the immense curve with his eyes into the shimmering distance. He had once hunted alongside the dark-skinned Ostrich-men who had two toes on each foot and ran like the Patthylyon-wind. They had laughed at him as he tried to keep pace with his huge, unwieldy frame. But they had also grown to respect him when, at the end of each day, he arrived, hours later, having tracked them through the dust.
Another occasion he had discovered a fellow Umbriani warrior; an Ottwhan outcast named Farro, half dead in the Kythruu Forest having been brutally savaged by some unknown beast. Brec stood vigil by Farro's side that night, waiting for his Manna to ascend into the Ottwhan after-where. Yet in the morning he watched, awed, as Farro threw back his cloak and stood, whole again in his bloodied rags.

Two nights later he witnessed another spectacle. Awoken by agonized howls, Brec discovered that Farro had grown a whole shin-length in height. His nails had blackened, thickened and curved like claws, and he turned his bright, sorrowful eyes on Brec, bayed like a wounded hound, and bounded off into the pitch weave of the nighttime forrest.

But the wall was something else entirely.

All through the cool night he marched, and yet, in the broad morning shadow of the wall, he found himself still no closer to either sea or sign of life.

Then the last wonder Brec would ever witness occurred:

Deeply fatigued, he sought to rest himself against the wall to consider his predicament, and in doing this he discovered there was *nothing substantial* to lean on. He simply fell through it, landing not on sand, but on soft, deep grass peppered with a bright efflorescence of tiny meadow flora. He could not help but laugh, as for some reason he had not once thought to touch the wall in his long night's journey. Reaching into the hide satchel at his hip, he found his gilt butterwine horn and removed the finely crafted white gold lid. He raised the vessel up to parched lips and, grateful, drank deep of the smooth liquor. He closed his eyes and savored the rich tannins, the berry and pepper flavors exploding across his expert palate. He felt amazing. Opening his eyes again he glanced down, smiling as he replaced the ornate lid of the drinking horn.

And then he noticed with a shock that his hands were not, in fact, *his* hands.

Dropping the horn he quickly got to his feet, gawping at the utterly alien, yet hauntingly familiar clothing he found himself wearing. It was not only the garments that were strange to him; it was his whole self; body and mind. He took out the small oval mirror that he somehow knew was nestling amongst other trinkets in the hip satchel and gazed into it. The face that looked back, though less broad, was recognizably his. Cold green eyes blazed beneath a strong, straight brow. The wild golden mane, that had so recently adorned him, was gone. His hair was shorn to the skin, little more than a shadow. The nose swept unbroken and equine, and he wore a short, sculpted chin-beard and fine loops through both ears. Most striking of all was the thin scar that crossed his forehead in a diagonal line until it cut through his left brow then reversed back on itself, through his lips until it terminated, right of his chin. He touched it gently, wondering how he had received such a wound. Why he could not remember it.

He was, however, glad to discover a long slender blade sheathed in an elegant scabbard at his left hip. The tough black leather jerkin and leggings were of an exceptional quality, and his right arm was sheathed in a remarkably crafted silver plate armor. It appeared to mimic the working of his muscles and danced with glowing cyan slithers - alchemical flares from precious inlaid minerals.

"Shit." He whispered to himself. "I Forgot. Again..."

II

The city of Tantrix-Alumnae glowed like a caged aurora. Bathing the low clouds above in a dull golden light, it nestled comfortably in the foothills of the Ornisbach. Brec's name upon *this* world - this planet called Ardden - was Hergal Ban Egan, and he felt unbidden tears dampen his eyes as he gazed down upon it. Tantrix-Alumnae was a favorite of his many homes. Not the largest of cities, nor the most resplendent, he yet thought it the most beautiful - though from where he stood one would think that unlikely. The city wall was rutted and inelegant, rising out of the ancient landscape like a shear crag two hundred and fifty spans in height. It curved away from him in both directions, a coarse arc to oval the city; the imposing casing of the jewel within. Black smoke rose in slowly burgeoning gouts, like giant spectral fungi, from enormous vents and chimneys. It spread out across the sky lending a purple hue to the failing twilight.

Hergal was starting to feel extremely fatigued after the initial exhilaration of his return had passed. It was ever the way. But he could not allow himself the luxury of sleep. Not yet. The fast fading memories he had gathered in half a lifetime, as the man called Brec, had to be sifted through. The important elements had to be firmly secured in his mind if the experience was to have any purpose at all. He also had be be careful how he managed his newly emergent memories of Ardden - dancing between the twin sets to create a new whole.

He felt giddy on relief and confusion.

Between Tantrix-Alumnae's great outer-wall, and the first of several lesser inner-walls, there was Pontifrax Parade. A wide panoply of cloistered shops; free houses and opiate spas. Hergal decided to seek out "the Sayer's Alms". An old, unselfconsciously decadent haunt in the western reaches of the Parade, it was one of the first places on Ardden he could clearly recall. A good place to review his situation, he judged.

At Methen's gate he sought out a Guardsman, barely noticing the desperate crush of people. They petitioned for access with official looking documents, earnest desperation, or bribery. A very few might slip unobtrusively through in the midst of the melee, but most would fail. The amassed fortunes of the Island's wealthiest citizens had been proffered for a slice of real-estate within Tantrix-Alumnae's walls; to little avail. It was a proud city burgeoning with a host that could often recount their generational heritage back over a thousand years. They would give up their birthright only at the very last, clinging to their meagerly apportioned acreage as though it were the only thing that sustained them.

Hergal reached inside his hip satchel for a certain Ornish artifact: A crude silver ring, far too large to wear, upon which was mounted a chunk of amber containing an ugly prehistoric beetle. It was priceless, and singled him out as somebody of import. There were no more than twenty of these rings in the city, and other notable denizens would bear a similarly priceless broach, or clasp or buckle - all decorated with a lump of amber within which some or other ancient creature had met a sticky end. He presented it to a Guardsman who hastily removed his iridescent blue crested helm and bowed.

He escorted Hergal swiftly through the mob, clearing a brief passage with shouts and shoves. The desperate hoard begged Hergal to help them, grabbed at him, pleaded - but he was soon through to Pontifrax Parade where the crowds thinned and the guardsman bid him good day.

Once inside the city Hergal could more clearly recall it's geography, as old familiarities awoke his long-slumbering memories. Concentric circular terraced parades echoed the outermost ring, like ripples in a pool; Peribold Walk, with its many-colored guest houses and ancient elms. Ardinax Street, with its ostentatious Banker's-Guild Hall, imposing granite facades. Penn and Willow Street crowded with a cacophony of artisans. Merchants and craftsmen competing for attention with brightly colored awnings, inventively manufactured signs. Finally, running up against the city's immense central inner-wall, there ran Duhn Ring, home to silk merchants, silver-smithies and other purveyors in the excesses of success. This vast wall was supported by five hundred and ninety-two flying buttresses. It reached vertiginous heights, four hundred spans and more. Light danced off the tough ground surface in faint swirls of azure and rose pearlescence. Within them lay the Old Town; the city proper. Here dwelt the descendants of the city's forefathers in archaic marble-veneered houses perched precariously on the top of Skaff Hill. None of the confusing rat-runs between the houses were named, though collectively they were known as the Flacks. (No one could remember why.) A final flint-cobbled wall ringed a small fortress and the tall Ornish temple at the city's apex.

Striding along the gentle curved walkway of Pontifrax Parade, Hergal glanced up at the snowcapped peaks of the Ornisbach, often called the "Aetuland Spine". A pale and unappreciable mass, it towered above Skaff Hill like some colossal fallen deity. These were the mountains that cut the island of Orn into two halves, neatly dividing Sutzeria, in the north, from Aetuland, in the south.

"Sutzeria." He thought to himself. "What's going on up there now?"

A large, simply carved sign in stained Cherry-wood spanned Pontifrax Parade and announced "The Sayer's Alms" to would-be patrons. The Inn had been built by the giant race of the Ornish many centuries earlier. It had once been a grain mill and warehouse and was massive when compared to the surrounding buildings - standing a third again as high, despite its being likewise constructed over three floors. A fresh coat of Mantis-green paint glistened on the ten-span oaken doors. The window-boxes overflowed with a cascade of vermilion and peach Porthalia, filling the air with their sharp sweet scent.

Inside, to Hergal's relief, the inn appeared mostly unchanged, though the plump Landlady was - not surprisingly - unfamiliar to him. Granite juts punctured the cream walls, which in turn supported a cross of broad oaken beams. These bore the weight of a complex wheel-like wooden structure, which splayed outwards from the center in elaborate curves, forming a platform upon which the upper floors now rested. All that remained of the original Ornish machinery.

"The Sayer's Alms" entertained a cosmopolitan host. A large breasted merchantess, with a sardonic bent to her forked smile, threw Hergal an inviting glance. He nodded in her direction, his clear eyes fixing on hers momentarily. A faint smile danced fleetingly across his lips, but he had other things to deal with before allowing such distractions to develop. Three local musicians pelted out a familiar shanty in the smaller adjoining bar - to hearty applause. The main bar was peopled with nobles, mercenaries, merchants and soldiers in the employ of city. They traded banter like blades. Others, practitioners of the Old Arts - alchemists, Fakkirs, philosophers and such - huddled at tables, arguing in hushed tones. Reconstituting abstractions and theorems in new, exciting variations. A palpable divide had grown between them and the nobles, it seemed. But the city's traditions were holding. Any bar room brawls would have seen the perpetrators cast out of Tantrix-Alumnae indefinitely, and that was more than either the nobles or alchemists were prepared to risk. Disagreements could be dealt with outside in the courtyard if it came to it. There was a designated square for violent confrontations at all of Tantrix Alumnae's inns, but losers faced possible exile and the squares had become more symbolic than anything else.

A Soul-less Ornish mercenary towered gloomily in a dim corner, his tattoos charting his downfall. He appeared to be looking for someone, his tragic violet eyes briefly settling upon Hergal before restlessly flitting on.

Hergal settled himself in a hermit-stall opposite the crackling central fire, and ordered a long ale and a Merchant's Platter. As Brec, beer - not wine - had been his drink of choice, and that part of him still fought for dominance. He was finding it hard to come to terms with the plain reality of the situation: He did not, as Brec, truly exist anymore. For thirty-four years he had been that other man. The powerful mercenary in the bearskin, famed across three continents! Hergal looked at his manicured fingers with distaste. These were the hands of a poet, not the hard-come-by hands of a warrior! Though he was in fact a highly accomplished swordsman, he had grown accustomed to Brec's thuggish barbarism. He mourned the loss of a life more simple.

The platter and the flames warmed him. He rediscovered the carved soapstone pipe, it's ornate mahogany stem inlaid with a silver thread. The pouch of aromatic Tobbach. He began to relax.

"Returning is never easy." He said to himself, like a mantra. "Try to remember that, the next time."

It took monumental self-discipline for Hergal to regard the larger sweep of recent events with a dispassionate eye. What had been going on in Aetuland since he had been away? He was back again, but what - if anything - had been learnt in this foray? What had he achieved by undertaking it?

He waved over to the barmaid, who's name, he had discovered, was Mola. It was early, and his taste for expensive butterwine was returning.

III

Tunny Mal-Tuboly swung his booted feet up onto a stool, belched, and closed his eyes, luxuriating in the warm afterglow of a "Hero's Portion" and three ox-bladders of nettle wine.

"Not bad." He muttered contentedly to himself. "Not bloody bad at all."

Tunny was a stocky ball of improbable muscle. A dance of black coils spilled around his shoulders and was, along with two sparkling dark eyes rimmed by long curling black lashes, his only claim to beauty. A vast beard hid the remainder of his face.

"Mal-Tuboly? May we speak?"

Tunny stumbled, cursing, half to his feet, hand fumbling at his empty scabbard. No weapons were permitted in "the Sayer's Alms".

"Great Orn, man! Can't a fellow drink in peace any more?" he spluttered, red faced.

The Ornish Soul-less pulled back the stool, which had, moments earlier, supported Tunny's feet, and carefully sat down, so that he met the now standing man eye to eye.

"I did not wish to startle you, Mal-Tuboly." He said. "May I speak with you?"

The voice, as with all the giant Ornish, had the quality of sounding like many voices in unison. Even at little more than a whisper it commanded regard. Tunny scrutinized the enormous tattooed figure, perched precariously on the seemingly diminutive stool, with wary eyes.

"You're not from Thurford are you?" He paused. "You know, what happened in "The Fine Prospect" last night... Well, it wasn't really my fault old chap..."

The mercenary looked confused.

"No? Well, then. Good. Good. A sticky matter, best forgotten. No harm done."

The Ornish Soul-less gathered his brow, looking troubled. He stared down at his own huge hands, spreading them palms up as if he were looking for answers there, then abruptly balling them into two minutely shuddering clubbed fists. The vast man raised his wonderful, hairless head and met Tunny eye to eye again.

Tunny calmed, suddenly filled with compassion. He was, after all, a man of great empathy. It was a part of what made him so endearing. Before him sat an Ornish Soul-less - a child of that rare, ancient and most sacred race. The direct offspring, legend told, of the god who gave his name to the emerald island within which Aetuland and Sutzeria nestled restlessly: Orn.

And in the giant's eyes Tunny saw a profound sorrow that touched him instantly, snuffing out any misgivings.

"Right o." He said. "All right. Please. Go ahead."

The Soul-less looked over toward the window, beyond which - though they could not see it - lay the Ornisbach, and beyond that, Sutzeria.

He returned his gaze to Tunny.

"My name is Iutzparthi-Llud Pellaquial, though most know me as Pellaq. I am, as you see, an Ornish Soul-less, and a mercenary. I have been told you are well connected, Mal-Tuboly. That you might know where to find a man. I also have an offer you yourself might be interested in."

Tunny peered intently into his companion's gentle eyes.

"An offer, eh? And what might that be, old chap?"

Tunny was blessed with unusual skills in matters of the blade, though cursed with a rogue streak of cowardice. He found himself a wandering sword-for-hire. His nature suited only the briefest of loyalties. His bold declarations of honor, love or fealty were noisome and expansive, but they were sickly, and prone to wither. He was a dreamer, hoping to find something great in the world, something worthy of his life; his death. He was, however, the heartiest of companions and enjoyed a peculiar kind of fame throughout Orn. There was hardly a man of consequence he had not known, however fleetingly. His gift was to be beloved of almost all who met him - and a kind of small magic there was in that.

"I do not wish to go into all the details now. It is a fragile matter. However, the man whom I seek is one Woebeg Ban Egan."

Tunny's eyes narrowed.

"I may have heard of the fellow. Then again... Perhaps I haven't. It would help if I knew your particular interest in him. It might help me, shall we say, narrow it down a bit?"

The Ornish Soul-less took a deep breath and stroked his bald pate with his vast left hand.

"Suffice it to say that regarding Ban Egan, his skills as a fighting man are famed, and that is what we seek. Warriors. The finest. You have a certain fame yourself in swordsmanship, Mal-Tuboly. There is a Hefty payment for what we propose."

Tunny nodded his fat round head gently.

"Give me a couple of days, all right chap? I'll see what I can do."

IV

Bloodrushinglikewindfirecoldnotnocannotcannotlikerunningrunningruinruinoustothebrightonedo wndowndowntotheseatoOrnwhowillalwaysbethereattheendalwayswaitingwaitingandrunningIamr unninghurtandpainpainlikefirecoldhotbloodbloodandIdidIdiditandithurtsohOrnihurts...

I'm shaking and I can't see properly, and there's a monologue running in my head, falling through my head, that's taking my mind off the pain. I think I've lost my left arm but I can't be sure, there's no time to look, no time to stop the blood that must be pouring, gushing. I'm screaming like Thotlan, and the blade that writes the Karnak in the air should be a two-hander, but she sings beautifully all the same. Bloody vapor trails her passing, clotting my nose, I breath through a grin; a grim grin. And the faces are (scared/angry/mad/sad) all exactly the same, the same face, cut in two, in half, like fruit, an opening, so slowly, like a red bloom, in a cheek, an eye. Small explosions of crimson, bursts of salty metallic blood-sweat-tears. Clawing pleading hands. I'm laughing because it's the best they've got, the very best. And it's not enough because I'm nearly there and they can't stop me. They can't stop me. And the last ones run as I open their friend/brother/comrade neck to groin, shoulder to hip, wide open, like a flower, a big bright flower opening, red, facing the sun, opening up to the sun.

And I'm out, I'm out, and I'm laughing/crying blood sweat tears...

Hergal awoke violently to sodden sheets and an unfamiliar ceiling. A young noblewoman, whom he did not immediately recognize, stroked his forehead gently. Mewing. He felt a knot of distaste writhe in his guts. Though not physically unattractive, the girl was blemished by a smug, patronizing air which hung about her like old sweat. She pouted in a manner that only contrived to intensify Hergal's sudden distrust of her. Her narrowed eyes were too full of questions. He bemoaned his lack of better judgment having consumed far too much alcohol the previous evening.

"Leave." Hergal whispered.

"Are you all right? You were dreaming..."

"I was dreaming. Now I am awake. Please do as I ask, and leave."

Any pretense at liking Hergal vanished in a cold instant from the girl's eyes. She stood, quickly, flaunting her nudity like a weapon, her pert breasts jutting below a similarly jutting chin. "So, you're just going to kick me out? No breakfast, no kind words? Did I do something wrong, Hergal? Or was I just a fuck? You were certainly happy enough to bring me here last night!"

Hergal set his teeth, but did not hide the frost in his eyes. "I've got too much to think about right now. My head hurts, and I'm sorry, but I have no recollection of what I said to you last night, or how we got to be here! If you wish, please, write me your address - and I'll maybe get in contact. Right now though, I'd really just like to be alone."

The flustered girl started gathering up her clothing, flung carelessly over a wooden chair and strewn in ribbons and bunches across the floor. "Well, you're definitely not the same man I met last night..."

"That" said Hergal "is certainly fucking true enough."

Later, emerging from the tastefully modest little guesthouse on Peribold Walk, Hergal pondered darkly the dream - a phantom memory? - that had awakened him. It caused him to rub subconsciously at his left arm beneath the elbow. He still sweated lightly.

"So, you are back to bother me some more, eh?" He thought gravely to himself. "Nuddfegh Ho."

Barachal Tush, the Sayer, found Tantrix-Alumnae much changed. Whilst Sayers had always induced a little fear in the human citizens of the city, and distrust in the Ornish, the outright disgust he now encountered on the streets verged on the alarming. His golden robes were spattered with gobules of spit. Inn doors were noisily barred shut at his passing as word sped up the streets that a Sayer was amongst them. It grieved him enormously. He took it all as a sign that the Tells were right. That what he had gleaned in the Echoes-To-Be was coming to pass.

He knitted his gold and black furred brow into furrows. He was here at least. And those he sought - those whose futures would impact on that of the planet Ardden, on that of the very universe they all dwelt within - they were here also. Now. With the fate of uncountable billions of lives resting heavily on his shoulders, such dark murderous looks as Tantrix-Alumnae's ignorant populace cast him were of little consequence. He continued his troubled search through the streets, and, to the extent he was able, paid their populace no heed.

"A word, if you please..." a young male voice barked suddenly, at Hergal's left. To his right another older man appeared, and Hergal was aware of at least two more people behind him.

"I'm in a hurry," growled Hergal. "Speak as we walk, if you must."

"If you are obliging, sir Munger-lover, and allow us to escort you out through the Lion Gate, you will come to no harm. There have been changes in Tantrix-Alumnae since you disappeared. Your kind, my Lordt Warloc, are no longer welcome in Tantrix-Alumnae."

Hergal, frowning, turned to the younger man - a city noble by his dress and bearing, quite at odds with the accompanying thug.

"So. You know I'm a Lordt of Tantrix-Alumnae. You know my name." Said Hergal, "I would normally expect better manners from someone of your evident standing, but then I've been away for a while. Tell me then, how is it you know who I am? And why is it you choose to call me a "Munger-lover" and a "Warloc"?"

The youth wrinkled his nose in distaste. "I've spent some time this morning, shall we say, *researching* you, Lordt Ban Egan. And, do tell: Where *have* you been for so long, and yet not aged a day? We, here, know of your kind. These are modern times. Our times. As I see, you still favor the fashions of the Ornish. Quaint. It was a look my father embraced in his youth. My generation chooses not to look to the past. Indeed we would rid the city of those dark and dangerous ways it once embraced. Warlockery, all Munger associated trickery, are practices we are committed to purging from these lands. The Ornish themselves are not above our scrutiny, sacred or no. Let the shit-eating Nefarean scum be ruled by the fear of magic and it's like! We won't be so easily cowed. You see, we're armed with new knowledge, the surety - the cool clarity - that the world does not barter in dreams. This is a harsh and solid *reality* in which we live, and we will defend the honesty of that with steel and our lives. The practitioners of our enemies' dark arts are themselves our enemies, so say we sir. We watch all who return. We have eyes in all places. In sleep you damned yourself..."

Hergal burst open the older mans left eye with a ringed finger, then ducked as a thin blade sliced through the air above his head. He rolled lightly on the cobbled street and was up again. He spun around, sword, free of sheath, carving a blur of intricate patterns in the air. The young noble was shocked to find fine slits opening across his forehead and both cheeks, weeping red rivulets.

"A man's dreams are his own, not subject to the laws of this world, let alone this city." Said Hergal, a frost in his eyes, as he peripherally noticed his carnal companion of the previous evening fearfully backing her way through the gathering crowd with a hand over her mouth. Her eyes were wide with shock, and she pointed at him but could utter nothing. He cursed her silently. "I suggest you get your friend here some medical assistance." he hissed. "And I certainly hope you're paying him well, poor sod. Now then, I have been friend to Tantrix-Alumnae for longer than you can guess, and may it always be so. As for my whereabouts these last how-many years... That is none of your bloody business. But I'll tell you this: It was spent in service of this city, and this island, Orn. My age is my own concern - but, as you see; I take care of myself."

"Fuck you, Warloc! We'll get rid of your kind soon enough! We'll put you all to the fucking torch..."

Hergal's blade flashed again above the bridge of the noble's nose, pricking him. He stared along the blade's length, meeting the man eye to eye.

"I don't know you - not yet. But, if I were you, I would get out of the city. You have no idea who you're messing with. I don't forget faces, and yours has some - let's say - *distinctive* features now. I'll enjoy finding out who you are, what games you play here. And I'll relish hunting you down. Rest assured, your own ignorance will be your downfall. Now piss off, boy. I'm bored of this."

The man glared at Hergal, crimson blazing in his cosseted blood-streaked cheeks. A hand hovered uncertainly above his still sheathed sword. He seemed to be deciding on what his rejoinder might be - but then he grunted abruptly, gestured that the two others attend the injured man, and shouldered his way belligerently through the gathered onlookers dabbing a handkerchief at his bleeding face.

Hergal kept his sword poised and steady until they had all departed, then sheathed it in a manner more befitting a larger, rougher man - Brec's legacy. Bile burned his throat. A slight tremor danced up his spine, bristling the hairs on the back of his neck. Blood throbbed up around his temples.

Turning brusquely, Hergal marched to the next throughfare into Ardinax Street, where he puked against a wall. A short while after that he refreshed himself with a drink from one of the many spas, cleaning his bloodied hand and splashing his face in the naturally warm mineral water. Then he walked shakily on, via Penn and Willow Street and Duhn Ring, ever inward, arriving eventually at the Raven Gate - the only way into the Old Town.

Clearly the city was changing and he could not delay a meeting with his Ornish tutor and benefactor any longer. He would have to see Iutznefydd-Baal Pellafinn before he could plan his next move.

Pellafinn was four hundred and thirty-six years old. A High-Order Ornumnae priest, he had a vast wealth at his disposal, and he was well informed as to events in Sutzeria and Aetuland. He learnt what he could about movements, plots and power plays abroad on the continent - in Nefarea, Ypo-Polaria, the former Free Nochentia, and further west, Kushna and Urodochi – via free agents in his employ. Almost every nation had, over generations, been crushed by the Nefars in their grand sweeping raids southward. Aetuland would not remain free of their menace forever he feared.

"Pellafinn, you old bastard." croaked Hergal, as matter-of-factly as he could manage, "Still brooding over your maps I see..."

The Ornish priest raised himself up to his full seven spans - short for the Ornish - and turned, a little unsoundly, to face Hergal, standing framed in the enormous study doorway. Pellafinn regarded his student intently for perhaps the thousandth time, squinting myopic eyes, before customarily shaking his head. For many years - a hundred? More? - he had not much liked the man. He found Hergal's cold green eyes too full of secrets. His manner somewhat overbearing, arrogant. Above all, he had hated Hergal's vanity. However, too many decades and common causes had created a unique bond between them. Hergal, as far as Pellafinn was able to judge, was only a little less than seventy years younger than he, and time had eroded those sharper edges, as experience, in many forms, had heightened his regard for the other man. There was so little to marvel at in this age, and yet Hergal was a genuine wonder, a throwback to a time when magic had been commonplace. He intrigued the old priest. Tantalized him with his metamorphic, world-striding energies.

Perhaps a little vanity was understandable in such a being after all.

As for Hergal, the old Ornish priest was not only frustratingly recondite, but always caused him to feel mildly nauseous. (This was certainly exacerbated by Hergal's current condition.) Pellafinn was distressing in appearance, pallid and cadaverous. An abomination of that beautiful, blessed race. His sickly-yellow bones glowed dully beneath his parchment skin, and his blood, in its weak coursing through aged broken veins, was faintly palpable. The priest's eyes were ruddy brown in the whites, and his pupils exactly matched the color. They bulged, chameleon-like, from their hollows above sallow, sunken cheeks. Underneath an impressively long, crooked nose, a thin, blue lipped and under-bitten mouth chewed continuously on Tobbach, the reason for his blackened teeth. And lower, that strange double cleft chin, faintly trembling. The pronounced "Ponti's Pear", jiggling distractingly in his sinuous throat. Completing the horror was the deeply etched tattoo that covered the lower half of his bald head in swirls and dots and zigzag lines. No amount of finery in his dress could conceal his physical shortcomings. The fastidiously polished black leather jerkin just enhanced the look of entropic consumption in his arms. The satin pantaloons - also black but finely decorated with ornate, symbolic patterns woven in golden thread - the high, fur-lined buckled boots, all contrived to create an image more of terror than splendor. Hergal could hardly believe he had grown to love this hideous old man as though he was his own father.

"My Lordt Hergal Ban Egan, come in, come in." said Pellafinn with an ironic half smile. Hergal found himself startled and immediately drawn to Pellafinn's mellifluous voice, which somehow he always managed to forget about.

"You've been gone from us for seventeen of our Ardden years! Well now... Have you recovered anything of use? Um? Were you many years in that other place?"

Predictably, Pellafinn wasted no time on pleasantries. Hergal smiled, but when he spoke, it was with an air of sadness and waste.

"Seventeen years this time? I suppose I should have expected things to change in that time, but I never remember. I'm never prepared for that. Ah, Pellafinn, you are my only constant! What little I did learn, though, may have scant use this time, old friend. I've brought nothing back with me, except maybe a fraction more knowledge of land warfare, and a perception of what it is like to be a rougher man of a lesser intellect! I do know that the Great Powers continue to fade everywhere - right across the universe it would seem. On the planet I've just returned from I came across few wonders, less even than here. Indeed, having forgotten completely my true self - I was born into the body of an infant this time Pellafinn - in thirty-four years abroad in a another world, the greatest wonder I encountered was a vast wall! It appears the Kiazmus, "The Pathway Home", is hidden there in this guise. A huge featureless wall! This, in turn, was disguised as an uninhabited island. Given the ill-educated nature of most of it's people, great powers must have been skillfully tapped there once for such a work to be wrought. A superior understanding must have been fairly common once, you'd have thought, at some earlier age. And, yet again, I stumbled across it. The Kiazmus. Drawn to it in some way I can't even perceive. It always pulls me back here. I never get lost."

Turning his back on the man he had not spoken to for seventeen years - thirty four in Hergal's case, space and time being the complex things they are - Pellafinn cast his filmy eyes over yet more intricate charts.

"The Great Powers continue to fade? I had thought it must be so. All the signs suggested as much."

Hergal fought the rising urge to throttle the old priest for his apparent lack of interest in his story - a half a lifetime in another world!

"So." He said eventually, and with studied calm. "What's going on in Sutzeria, Pellafinn? Is it still free?"

"Ah. Yes." Replied the priest, not bothering to turn around. "Yes. You have got some catching up to do, haven't you?"

"Perhaps you would be so kind as to fill in the gaps for me then? Tantrix-Alumnae certainly has a different - edge to it."

Pellafinn carefully placed his precious charts in the wide shallow drawer of his plan chest and turned around to face Hergal at last.

"Since your departure, my dear young Hergal, there was - let me see - five years more peace before the Nefars yet again crossed the Sutzerean Straights. Tens of thousands of them sailed their Dragships up the river Rae to Duhn. And, yet again, the city fell. This time to great Ornish designed siege engines, I'm sorry to say. There are too many Soul-less Ornish mercenaries these days. Too many, by far. The 'new walls' only succeeded in delaying the agony I'm afraid. Another pointless tax for another pointless wall, which brought about another pointless famine in Duhn's poorer quarters! When will they ever learn? The army went east after that, as usual. Through the Forrest of Duhn, and on, parallel with the Ornisbach - the Aetuland spine. Within two weeks they arrived at Shea Pass and marched south to Da Derga's Heights..."

"Why do I know Da Derga's Heights?"

The small giant's eyebrows arched, eyes bulging incredulous below. "What? You do recall the Brookbane's famous Sutzerean castle-fortress? Surely you must?"

Hergal looked up at Pellafinn with an empty, tired expression.

"Just indulge me, you old fucker. My poor brain is still struggling with the reality of being back here!"

"Hm. Well. Very well. If you insist." The priest shook his large ugly head, collecting his thoughts. "Da Derga's Heights stand poised in the eastern most reaches of the Ornisbach, right on the Aetuland/Sutzeria boarder. It is, as I'm sure you will soon remember, an architectural achievement that remains unrivaled upon Ardden. There is no structure more famed - and you have been there in and out of my company on more than one occasion I can tell you..."

"Yes, I just can't... the memory - my memory - is all fucked up. Confused. It's returning, though somewhat painfully I have to say! So many holes..."

"One would not necessarily think it wise to go out drinking having recently journeyed between worlds, Hergal. You know, I've told you this before..."

Hergal waved a hand weakly and frowned.

"Enough! Enough bloody lectures Pellafinn! Just help me know where I am again - if that wouldn't be too much trouble..."

"Hm. Well, let's see. Let's see. Do you remember the Brookbane dynasty at all?"

Hergal shook his head slowly.

"Great Orn! What then, my dear Lordt Hergal Ban Egan, do you recall of Ardden? I can hardly tell you what you don't know if I don't know what you do!""

"Ouch. All right Pellafinn, this... is Tantrix-Alumnae."

The priest looked hard at Hergal, quite still for a moment, until it became clear he was not going to say any more.

"Am I to congratulate you on this remarkable achievement?" he spluttered. "Really now. And is there anything... else?"

"Orn's bollocks, Priest! I'm still two men! Two men! And I only have one sore head!" Hergal gathered himself and went on. "So, what I do know... what I know about, where we are... I know this: We are in the heart of Aetuland, which encompasses the southern half of this island, Orn. It is separated from the north, Sutzeria, by mountains. The Aetuland Spine - as I believe we in the south like to call... That lot, squatting out there..." Hergal gestured through the window vaguely. "I was thinking about it last night. Thinking about Sutzeria. What might be going on there. As for names, history - I confess it is all just a confusing blur.   The Empire of the Nefarians lies to the... *west* - I remember that - and it constitutes most of the continental mainland. Duhn is Sutzeria's largest city on the norwestern tip of the island..."

"Good. Then at least you should have understood what I have told you thus far!" The old giant sighed and resumed his story with the air of a teacher deeply displeased with an errant pupil. "This is all of immediate relevance to you, so listen carefully! I won't be most happy if I have to tell it twice. Time is of a high premium right now, Hergal, especially to the old. So. Lordt Thral ban Duhn Ne Brookbane - the rightful and last true ascendant of Da Derga's Heights - was a Sutzerean Warlordt by bloodline, but a well known Aetulander in his heart. He married, as has been the custom of centuries, a noblewoman from Aetuland. In his case, she was the Lady Pesheval Nar-Bo Tertrigal Ban Hapfthoven Ne Belorvelian-Alumnae..."

"How the fuck am I supposed to remember *that* Pellafinn?"

"Hergal, just listen. He met and, fortuitously, fell in love with The Lady Pesheval while studying here, at the Ornish temple in Tantrix-Alumnae. You drank in his company on a couple of occasions! I'd say you were close acquaintances, so you really ought to remember it!" Hergal frowned, rubbed his eyes. "The courtship was brief, intense and mutual I was told - by you as it happens. All concerned parties were content with the arrangement, and the union was compacted within a half year of their first meeting. They supposedly enjoyed three blissful years together before the Lady Pesheval became Munger-stricken and died over two long, agonizing weeks. Brookbane was heartbroken, and a certain wildness was reportedly noted in him thereafter. He remained, non-the-less, a fine Lordt to those that served or worked alongside him. Fair and generous to guest and friend, I believe, if a little dour when drunk. When Aetuland came under threat again it was he who organised and assembled the great army that gathered up there - the largest this land has ever hosted. He had put forth his argument at the Lordt's Council, reasoning that the plunging walls of the fortress had never been breached. That if Aetuland could be defended, then it would be best defended there: At Da Derga's Heights. Needless to say, the Lordts did not take much persuading. History was on the side of Da Derga's after all.

"The ensuing battle, now referred to as the 'Battle of Da Derga' - though Orn knows how many battles have been fought there! - lasted nearly three weeks before Lordt Brookbane splintered the Nefars with the assault that subsequently made him famous. The demoralized Nefars retreated, and Brookbane continued to harry them all the way back down the pass, until, tragically, a flaming arrow found its mark, blinding him. A good man he may well have been, but Brookbane was also, sadly, a *vain* man..." Pellafinn shot a pointed look at Hergal who was massaging his temples with the tips of his fingers, eyes shut. The giant sighed. "Something I fear all you so-called Lordts have in common - and that includes even you unlanded Lordts! So, accustomed to power, broken by tragedy, Brookbane was unable to accept his blindness. He vanished in the night, leaving his rivals to fight over Lordtsway of Da Derga's Heights.

"For the last twelve years there has been another uneasy peace between Aetuland and the now Nefarean occupied Sutzeria. Da Derga's Heights remains the only Sutzerean stronghold free of the Nefarean Empire's rule."

Pellafinn leaned slightly forward, his voice dropping. There was a conspiratorial glint in his muddy eyes that Hergal had, he realised, greatly missed.   "I have been hearing tall stories of late, Hergal. Disturbing stories." The clawed hands, with skin like oiled papyrous stretched over waxen bones, writhed in excitable knots around each other. How the priest loved his intrigue!   "There is a legend growing. A near mythic tale about a powerful Nefarean Warlordt. This Warlordt has won the favor of the Emperor and now holds sway over the Nefarians abroad in our lands. He operates from Duhn, it's said. Machivarius Point to be more precise. It is also whispered that he is a Warloc. That he can invoke the power of the Munger, the Undead God, through some fabled gemstone. It is rumored that he plans a new campaign to conquer Aetuland. They call
this man 'The Wayfarer.'"

"So. Well then. I have forgotten much. And it seems you are right, old man." Much had indeed happened since Hergal had been away. "I've some... catching up to do. What can we do about all this?"

"You'd do well to ask what I am already doing about it! You may be surprised to know that plans have been put in motion to try and steal the Gem of this 'Wayfarer', if such as it and he exists. So, Hergal. Let me ask you something: As one of the Ornish, I would lose my soul should I perpetrate any act of violence. Is it, therefore unseemly, do you think, for an Ornish priest to hire mercenaries?"

Epilogue

...donotforgetwhatwearrangedWayfareradealwasstruckadealdealinbloodyesyesyoua reminedonotforgetmineWayfarerWayfarertheTorctheTorcisminemustbeminethedealth edealthedealmustnotbebrokenyouaremineWayfarerdonotforget...

The Wayfarer fell to his knees, fearful and expectant.

The prospect of once again channeling energies long ago thought lost - too far from the physical world for any present day power to access them - chilled him. He shuddered. This was the cursed nature of his life now. Sweat gathered in the livid pitted holes that had once housed his eyes. He reached blindly forward with an unsteady but strong hand. Felt the edge of the ebony shrine. His stomach lurched, but he mastered it. Almost. Deftly he unhooked the elegant gold latch, swinging open the lid to reach inside. His fingers brushed against the padded silk that lined it - a deep vermilion had he been able to see - and fumbled around inside until they found, and closed upon, a smooth gemstone. It was almost exactly the size of an eyeball and was mounted within an intricate golden mesh and suspended from a thick white-gold chain.

Fervidly he fastened the chain around his neck and, laughing wildly, he jammed the gemstone into his right eye socket, rupturing the delicate flesh and causing blood to flow.

Moments later the rapturous agony of the gem's dark power surged upward through his spine. It exploded within his skull, slick and pitch, and burst out through the ruins of his eye sockets, around the edges of the stone - a bilious green flame which bathed the darkened room in a sickly light and lent him the one thing he most craved:

Sight.

Baalor Dark-Eye smiled bitterly.

13

SHERRIF 13

Ashley Wood | Artist |

www.ashleywoodartist.com

SEVENTY ONE

'74

SEVENTY FOUR
PTY LTD

SHERRIF 13

SHERRIF 13

SHERRIF 13

SHERRIF 13

SHERRIF 13

SHERRIF 13

SHERRIF 13

SHERRIF 13

SHERRIF 13

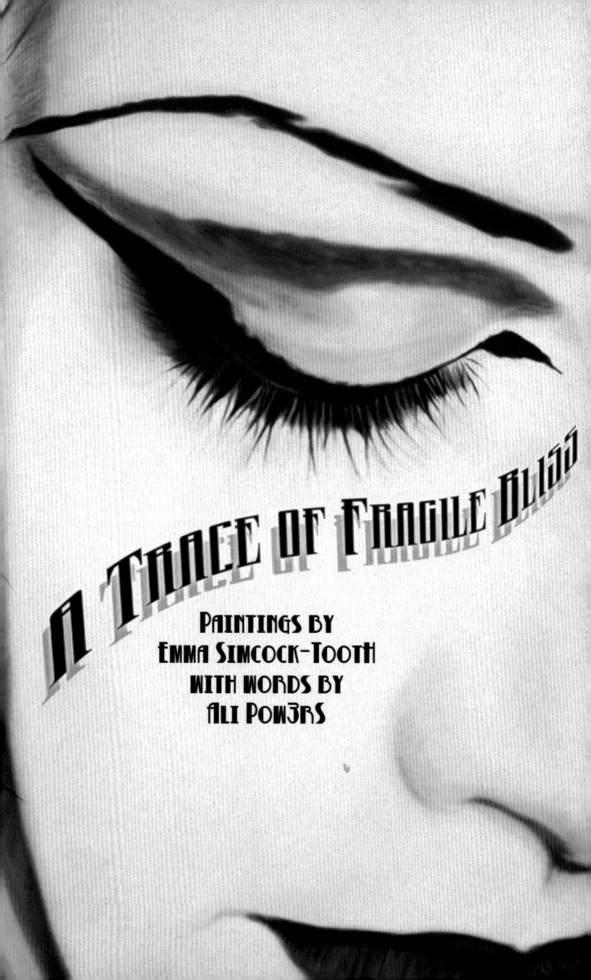

A Trace of Fragile Bliss

Paintings by
Emma Simcock-Tooth
with words by
Ali Pow3rs

People often think I'm a bit...

...self-obsessed.

A trace of fragile bliss.
Silken trails of wanting...
Wanting a miracle perhaps?
A pedestal, away from false attention?

But that's not quite how it is.

I think that we're all... you know... working OUTWARDS. And what we ARE is only half the answer.

Did you ever get caught in a circular dream? I did...

True reflections come
when stripped of reason,
pure as any martyrs play,
testing outright every note
that was ever in the way.

It's like falling down an UP escalator - I imagine there's one of those in hell! Always falling, never reaching the bottom...

Anyway, like I said, I don't think of it as self-obsession. Just working outwards...

I succumb to this new Kingdom
like the healing bodies breath .
Honey suckle air in winter's
soon forgotten death...

End.

Trip – Tick

By Gary Erskine

Story: Shane McCarthy

Art: Cardinal

THE CURE

IT'S CLOSE.

I CAN FEEL IT.

WHOLE BODY
ACHES LIKE HELL.

GUTS

ARE *KILLING* ME.

IT'S THE LAST ONE AND IT'S BIG. BLOODY *TYPICAL*.

STAGE THREE FOR SURE. BETTER NOT BE A FOUR...
LET'S FACE IT, IF IT'S A FOUR I'M WELL AND TRULY

Fucked.

ONE TO GO, ONE TO GO.

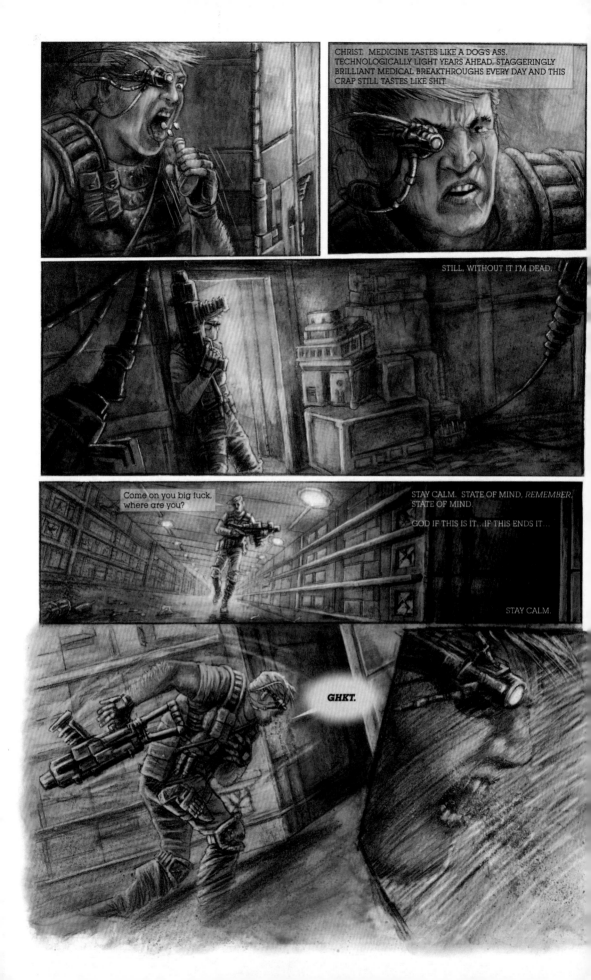

Christ...

FUCK *THIS*.

LAB BOYS'LL KILL ME FOR THIS...LIKE I GIVE A SHIT.

ONE MORE AND I'M HOME. GOD, JUST ONE MORE AND I'M OUT OF THIS HELL HOLE.

Christ! Just look at it.

BUT IN THE END? DISEASE. FOUL, VICIOUS, PENETRATING DISEASE.

ALL THIS BROUGHT ABOUT BY SOME INSANE GOVERNMENT SCIENTIST THAT DECIDED TO SAVE THE WORLD.

IT COULD HAVE BEEN ANY NUMBER OF THINGS; WAR, FAMINE, DICKLESS BOY BANDS...

BROUGHT TO OUR KNEES LIKE A CHEAP WHORE UNTIL SOME FUCKER FINDS A WAY TO "LEVEL" THE PLAYING FIELD.

THEY LIKEN HUNTING THESE THINGS TO CLIMBING A MOUNTAIN.

MONTHS OF TRAINING AND PREPARATION, ENDLESS HOURS OF LECTURING AND SPECIFICS ON EQUIPMENT

AND IN THE END IT'S ALL DOWN TO ONE MAN DESPERATELY TRYING TO MAKE THE DISTANCE.

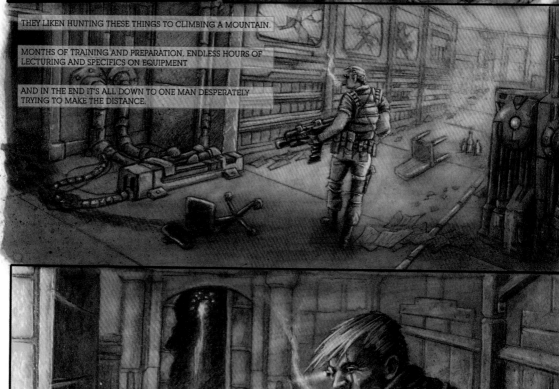

ONE MAN AGAINST A MOUNTAIN.

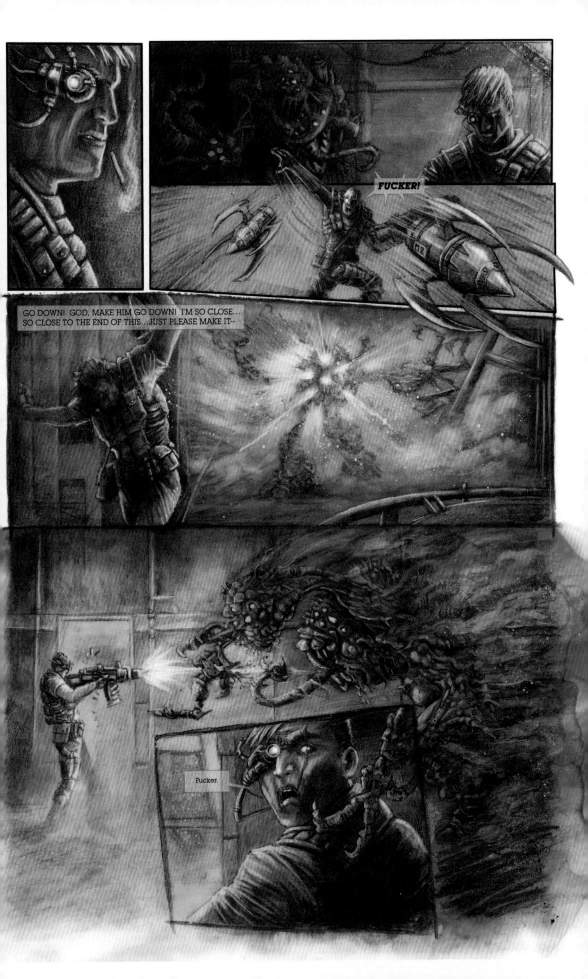

"FIELD SURGEONS" THEY CALL US. THEY THINK IT'S FUNNY. BUNCH OF SMART ASS SCIENCE BOYS.

SENT HERE TO CUT THESE THINGS OUT.

IT MADE LOGICAL SENSE TO SOMEONE.

GIVE HUMANS A GUN AND WE CAN KILL ANYTHING. GIVE US SOME MICROSCOPIC PIECE OF SHIT AND WE'RE STUMPED.

HATS OFF TO THE DICKHEAD WHO THOUGHT MAKING CANCER INTO A TWELVE FOOT GIANT WITH A TEMPER PROBLEM WAS A FUCKING GOOD IDEA

ANSWER? GIVE IT A FACE AND WE'LL BLOW IT OFF.

SMART.

Boy scouts...

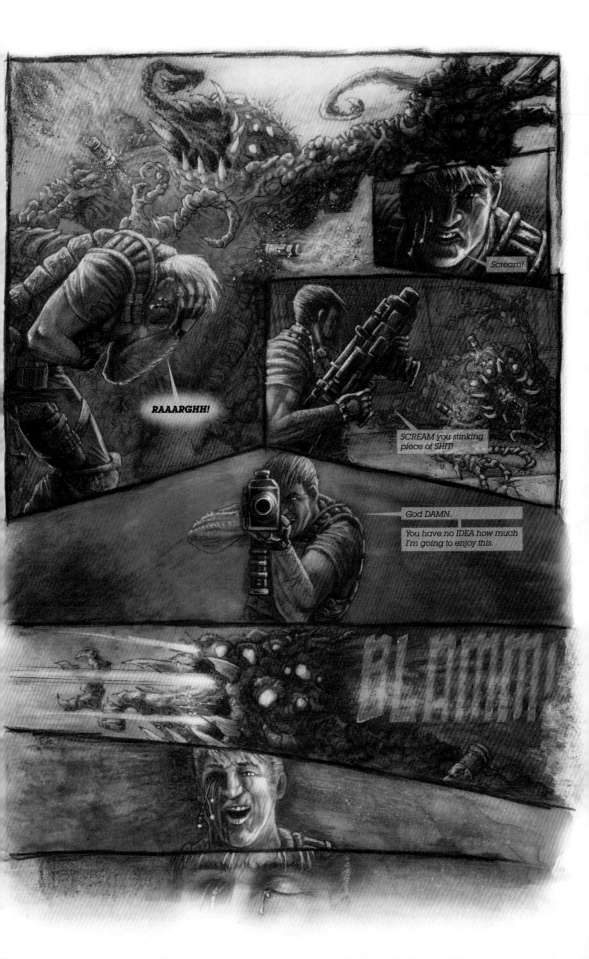

Ali Powers WORDS
Samuel Araya ART

The Wormcast

I am a Hopper, author of "The Transient", 4th dimensional
prophet (2nd class) in the 5th century of the New Time.
What you are reading is a Zenopod,
a time capsule of the eternal.

This is the future of mankind...

All war has ceased.

All calendars have been re-written by the order of the
sun and the moon, their eclipses guiding us out
of the darkness to live in the infinite.

Parchment - no longer sourced as it once was by the divi-
nation of forests - is grown as a luminous cell-structured
synthetic compound, retaining the imprint of thought by
truly understanding the nature of thinking. The 'con-
jured', and the 'captured' are born equally in this logical
framework, which exists as it did even in your time.

None of this was fully understood until 'Her', the divine
one. Never has life bloomed in such abundance.

How it is possible and how all this came to be
I will explain.

It all started as a simple joke, a gesture to un-write the
book, and then rewrite it as a single picture, to join tho
pictures together like plastic cup telephones or flick bo
animations. But it ended up revealing the basic law
and pace of the entire universe, and in doing so
formed a new society...

The 'Never Awake Movement' took over, from the gra
roots up, and the most basic of fundamental misconce
tions unravelled in the breeze - just as men unravelled
the sight of "Her", our new Venus.

So what changed? What prompted this reckoning?

The liars ran out of excuses. The dreamers pursued the
visions until they were finally realised.

The world came to a crossroads:

By early July 2015 man's pursuit of the distant stars dwindled. No longer were we able to reach so far. Gaia's arm was weak, gasoline was low, and the air was as thick as gravy in a hot tub. New technology surfaced when willful genetic manipulation of the organism did little to manipulate the organism's will.

Chance still played the greater role in development than origin did. But as science and psychology joined hands, test subjects were born manufactured. Orchestrated forgeries of the human animal, all with basic genetic traits understood.

These 'babies' grew within closed societies where all actions were monitored peacefully by implanted 'Nanodrones'. These conveyed everything - from pulse rate to hormone release - into the spiralling central database, all working to the decaying of time, as it was understood at that time (gravity, and motion towards the Event Horizon).

Soon it was recognised that the manifestation called "reality" was of man's own making, and was the only "reality" man had ever known.

Time passed. We continued to live inside the nightmare we had made for ourselves. 'Geo-Tech' maintained control over the patented process of "Air Recycling and Distribution". But as successive generations grew up it became increasingly clear how to adjust every nuance of the world. Climate change was first monitored, then turned back, by giant mechanical waterspouts controlled by geo-synchronous satellites. Part machine, part living extension of planet Earth, these redistributed everything, from water vapour in the atmosphere to the very winds themselves.

Dreams walked beside us and breathed the air from our lungs. We breathed because they existed with us.

The test subjects grew, as did our understanding of them, and by 2376 it became clear that space-time could now be modified. It was long understood the 'perception' of time could be radically altered simply by temperature variation. Now, due to the astonishing conclusions drawn from what could only be called the 'results' of the experiment, we could actually venture even closer to a full understanding:

By delaying certain hormones in the subject, their lifestyle was altered. Dependence on other features of the eco-system was changed, and by cloning certain elements of that 'moment' in the eco-system new patterns emerged later in the loop of that ecosystem. Realising what we had done we attempted to reverse the inevitable, but failed.

Then 'The Archaeologist' made a startling discovery:

Deja Vue.

Have you wondered how precognition could be possible?
Or even how you know what you think you know
in the first place?

It was first called 'Genetic Superstition' by a failing of logic, then 'False Awakening' because of a 'dream/world imbalance'. They were cast off as media hoaxes, but one by one they appeared.

And no other conclusion made sense anymore.

The first artefact was 'The Wormcast'. The ship was just being built at the same time it was discovered adrift off the coast of Mexico. Everything from the name, the layout of the cabins to the carpet in the lobby was identical.
Then it went even further: The finding of future vessels - before their creation.

And then came the cities.

No future is required anymore, as it once was.
Balance and harmony is perfect in our age, but it's only by your discovery that this shall all come to be...

And this is why I commit this Zenopod to the ground, for in my time you have already found it.

Hopper
Omega Squared
Author of The Transient
Prophet 2nd Class

ONEIRONAUT

Written & Illustrated by Tom Muller

DESIGNED BY

Muller

ONEIRONAUTICS inc.

Discovering Reality since 1974

INTERNAL REPORT ● REALITY ACCESS: CROSSOVER SESSION 06031986*****B7 ●

> ANALYSIS REPORT:
 ● SESSION DOCUMENTED BY DR. ~~████████████████████~~

******06031986/ENTRY******

TODAY'S PROBE WAS SUCCESFUL. I CAN BARELY BELIEVE WE BROKE TROUGH. MY THEORIES... MY FEARS... THEY'RE CORRECT.
EVERYTHING IS A DREAM. OUR 'REALITY'... WAKING LIFE, IT'S AN ILLUSION. *EVERYTHING* IS A PROGRAMMED ILLUSION, A VIRTUAL
REALITY EXPERIENCE CREATED BY OUR OWN PERCEPTION.

EVERY MORNING WE WAKE UP WE START DREAMING. WE WAKE UP FROM OUR *REAL* REALITY.

OUR PERCEPTION OF REALITY IS DICTATED BY OUR PERCEPTION. OUR EYES WORK AS REFLECTOR DISHES.
LIGHT REFLECTS ON EVERYTHING AROUND US, THOSE REFLECTIONS GET TRANSMITTED TO OUR BRAIN TO BE DECODED/RECODED BY OUR VISUAL CORTEX
INTO SOMETHING OUR BRAIN CAN COMPREHEND. IN FACT ALL WE 'SEE' IS LIGHT REFLECTED. OUR BRAIN GIVES IT FORM.

>----------------------------
FIRST SIGNS THAT SUPPORT MY THEORY AROSE WHEN WE STARTED RECEIVING REPORTS OF INDIVIDUALS WHO APPEARED TO BE ABLE TO CONTROL
THEIR DREAMS IN 1967. THE SURGE IN POPULARITY OF MENTAL STIMULANTS LIKE L.S.D IS ATTRIBUTED TO THE DISCOVERY (***SEE FILE HA07/B0028).
>----------------------------

EARLY INTERVIEWS WITH SAID SUBJECTS AND BETA TESTING REVEALED THAT THE SEEMINGLY DREAM-LIKE IMAGES AND SITUATIONS THEY EXPERIENCED
WERE REAL, AND ALLOWED THEM TO 'ESCAPE' INTO REALITY FULLY AWARE. ****************** AS A FAILSAFE MEASURE TO AVOID WIDESPREAD PANIC
L.S.D. WAS MADE ILLEGAL*****************.

FURTHER RESEARCH SHOWED THAT THIS ABILITY IS DORMANT IN EVERYONE. BUT WITHOUT OUTSIDE HELP, 'CLEAN' SUBJECTS DON'T SEEM TO BE ABLE
TO ACCESS REALITY.

WHEN WE SLEEP WE ARE IN A STATE OF FLUX, ABLE TO ACCESS REALITY. IN OTHER WORDS: WE HAVE THE ABILITY TO WAKE UP.
HEREIN LIES THE PROBLEM: OUR BRAIN IS UNABLE TO DECODE AND INTERPRET THE SIGNALS IT RECEIVES. INPUT GETS MISFIRED AND WE RECEIVE
FRAGMENTED/SURREAL AND ELUSIVE IMAGES, WE THEREFORE THINK WE'RE IN A DREAMSTATE.

===

NOW. WHEN YOU GO TO BED AT NIGHT, AND CLOSE YOUR EYES, YOU SEE NOTHING. ITS BLACK, AND YOU START SEEING BRIGHT COLORS, SHAPES,...
THINGS YOU CAN'T DESCRIBE - AND YOU START DREAMING. OR SO YOU PERCEIVE. IN ACTUALITY YOU'RE WAKING UP. THE DREAMS ARE YOUR LIFE,
REAL REALITY, BUT BECAUSE YOUR BRAIN DOESN'T REALIZE ITS ACTUALLY AWAKE, THE SIGNALS GET ALL DISTORTED AND DECODED WRONG.
THATS WHY DREAMS SEEM SO ERRATIC AND ELUSIVE. WHEN YOU 'WAKE UP' AGAIN IN THE MORNING, YOU CAN BARELY REMEMBER WHAT HAPPENED.

===

WE FINALLY HAD A BREAKTHROUGH. FOR YEARS WE'VE BEEN DEPLOYING ONEIRONAUTS, HOPING TO GET A GLIMPSE OF WHAT OUR REALITY LOOKS LIKE.
WE'RE HOPING TO FIND A WAY TO CROSS OVER. TO INVERT COMPLETELY.

OUR FRIENDS AT STANFORD U. DEVELOPED A PIECE OF SOFTWARE THAT ENABLED US TO RECORD THE FIRST REALITY BARRIER.
THE RESULTS ARE TOO OVERWHELMING. THE IMAGES WE RECEIVED WILL HAUNT US FOR SOME TIME.
(******** SEE ATTACHED DOCUMENTS ********)

**************************** /BARRIER 01 CAPTURE

```
> ENTRY: B01_A

> CONTINUE? [Y/N]
>[YES]
>
>
RUN_
```

```
                                    > *** WARNING! ***
                                    > *** WARNING! ***
                                    > *** WARNING! ***
                                    > *** WARNING! ***
                                    > *** WARNING! ***   > INPUT OVERLOAD
```

```
> COMPENSATING...
> COMPENSATING...
>
>
>     LOADING BUFFER PROGRAM 01...
>     INITIALIZING BUFFER PROGRAM 01...
>
>
>     COMPENSATING FEEDBACK SIGNAL...
>     BUFFER PROGRAM 01 RUNNING...

------------------------------------

> CONTINUE_
```

THE ENTRY WENT WITH THE USUAL BUMPS. ONCE THE SUBJECT STARTS SLEEPING/WAKING UP THE SIGNAL
GETS BOOSTED BY 134.8%. THE IMAGE FEEDBACK IS POWERFULL: RANDOM SHAPES AND COLORS CREATE A
VORTEX, REACHING A CRITICAL MASS.
> MANUAL CLASSIFICATION REPORT ●
LIKE A MIRROR EFFECT THE SIGNAL REVERSES ITSELF AND
CALMS DOWN INTO A SOFT FLOW ONCE THE SUBJECT PASSES INTO A 'DREAMLIKE' STATE,
SLOWLY GETTING ACCUSTOMED TO THE ENVIRONMENT.

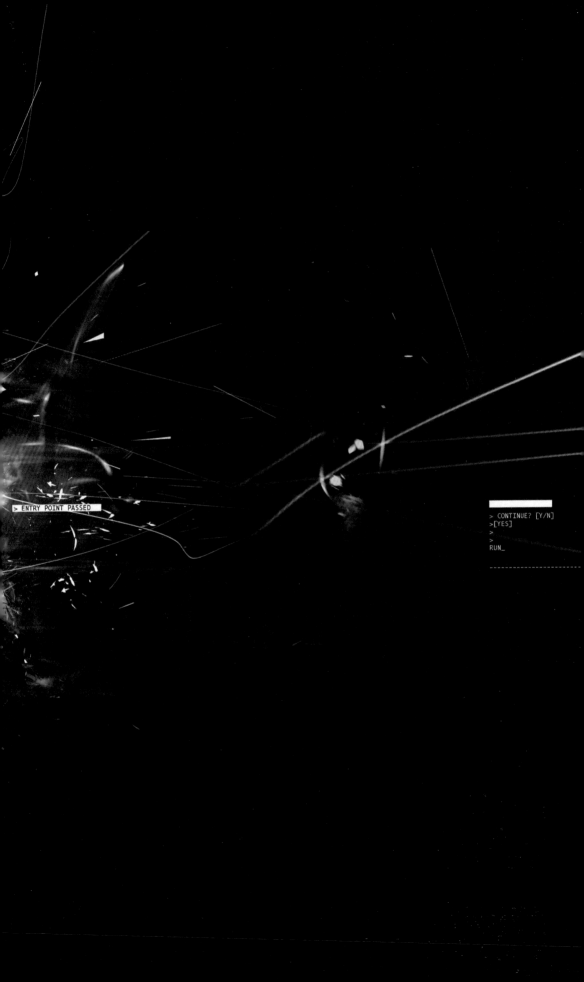

> ENTRY POINT PASSED

> CONTINUE? [Y/N]
>[YES]
>
>
RUN_

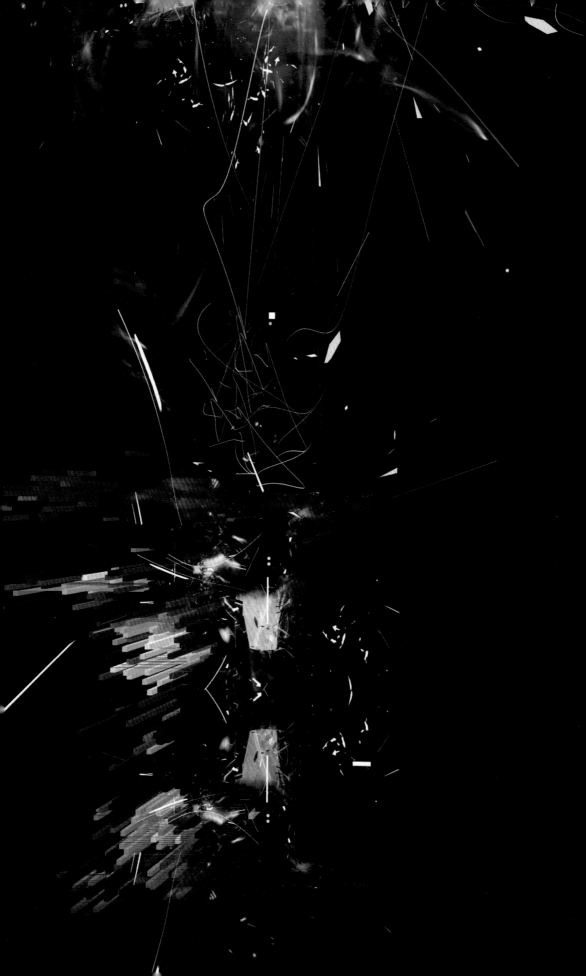

SUBJECT IS BECOMING FULLY AWARE OF REALITY. ENERGY PULSES RAGE AND RACE.
WHAT I CAN DESCRIBE AS NEUROSYNAPTICAL CURRENT SURGES FROM LAYER TO LAYER - SLOWLY UNFOLDING
FLOWER-LIKE STRUCTURES SEEMINGLY CONSTRUCTED FROM LIGHT.

```
> CONTINUE? [Y/N]
>[YES]
>
>
RUN_
```

THE 'FLOWER' (FOR LACK OF A BETTER DESCRIPTION)
SEEMS TO ACT AS A CATACLYST TO REBUILD
THE SUBJECT IN ACTUAL REALITY.

> CONTINUE? [Y/N]
>[YES]
>
RUN_

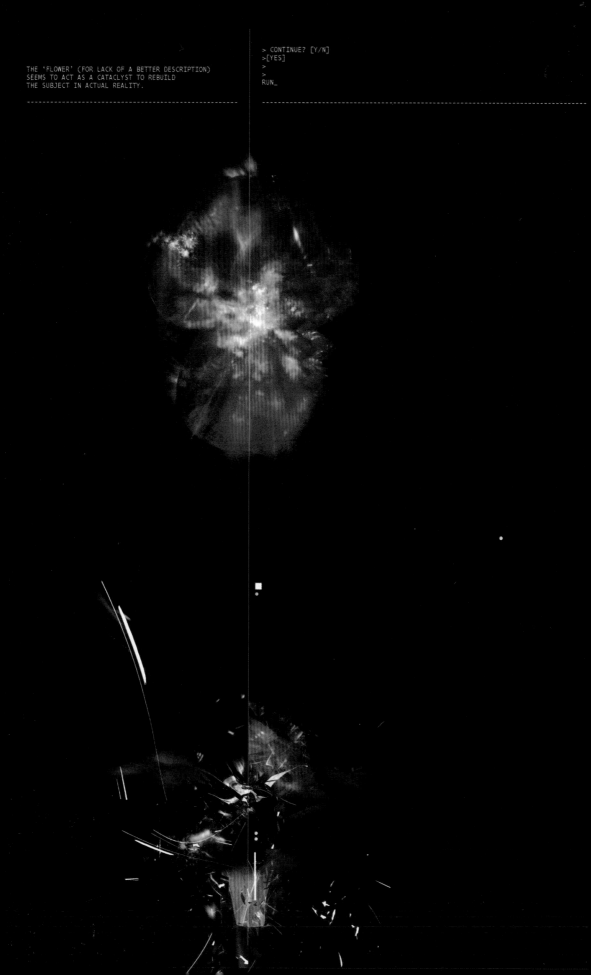

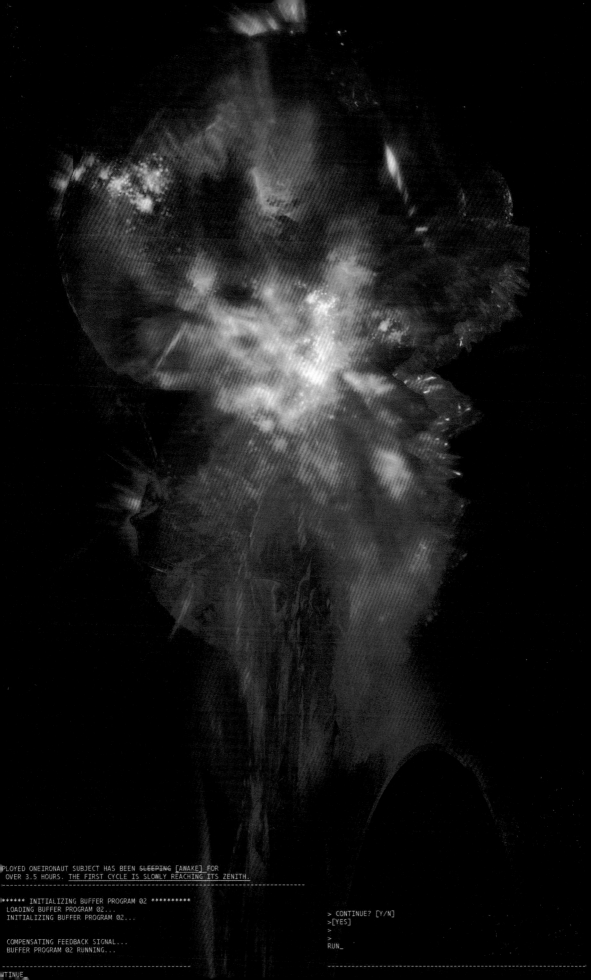

PLOYED ONEIRONAUT SUBJECT HAS BEEN ~~SLEEPING~~ [AWAKE] FOR
OVER 3.5 HOURS. THE FIRST CYCLE IS SLOWLY REACHING ITS ZENITH.

****** INITIALIZING BUFFER PROGRAM 02 **********
  LOADING BUFFER PROGRAM 02...   > CONTINUE? [Y/N]
  INITIALIZING BUFFER PROGRAM 02...   >[YES]

                                                            >
  COMPENSATING FEEDBACK SIGNAL...   RUN_
  BUFFER PROGRAM 02 RUNNING...

TINUE

```
> REND.ERROR   : BATCH PROCESSING FAILURE 0001/A
-----------------------------------------------------------------------------------------

> *********************** ABORTING SIGNAL************************
> *********************** ABORTING SIGNAL************************
> *********************** ABORTING SIGNAL************************

   --------------------------------------------------------------------------------

> ●                     ** SIGNAL ABORTED **
>    END RECORDING [Y/N]
> [YES]
>
>
>
>    RECORDING SESSION STOP / 00100.05:23

>    END PROGRAM_ ■
```

ONEIRONAUTICS inc.

Discovering Reality since 1974

INTERNAL REPORT ● REALITY ACCESS: CROSSOVER SESSION 06031986*****B7 ●

> ANALYSIS REPORT:

● SIGNAL LOST AT 00100.05:23

******FAILURE TO BREACH THE SECOND REALITY BARRIER******

AGAIN THE PROBE FAILED UPON REACHING THE 2ND BARRIER. ONCE THE SUBJECT STARTS TO BECOME FULLY AWARE THE SIGNAL IS
LOST. THE REASON STILL ELUDES US. THE PROGRAM RUNS AT 100% EFFICIENCY.

THE ONLY POSSIBLE EXPLANATION COULD BE THAT OUR BRAIN STILL HAS PROBLEMS INTERPRETING THE SIGNALS, AND ABORTS THE SIGNAL TO
AVOID INPUT OVERLOAD, WHICH MIGHT RESULT IN A COMATOSE/CATACONIC STATE... (****** SEE FILE CAT/01B5209).

STILL, THE RESULTS SO FAR GIVE US ENOUGH MATERIAL TO STUDY FOR NOW, BUT THE PAINFULL REALIZATION THAT ALL THIS, ALL THE THINGS
WE'RE DOING ARE JUST A FIGMENT OF OUR IMAGINATION... AN ILLUSION. IT MAKES ONE WONDER.

===

TIRED... I HAVE BEEN WORKING ON THESE LATEST FINDINGS FOR A MONTH NOW. WITHOUT ANY APPARENT BREAKTHROUGH.
I'LL BE RESUMING ANALISYS IN 72HRS, AFTER I'VE HAD SOME SLEEP.

*** END REPORT ***

START RECORDING_ ■

JOHN BAMBER WORDS   ART JOHN HOWARD

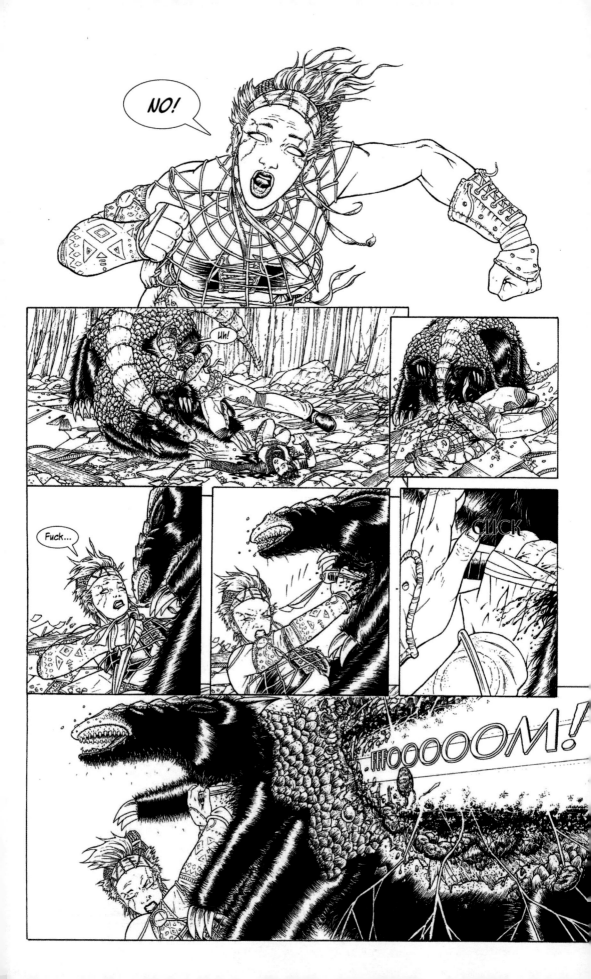

Only the PURE may walk this path.

Now we are ready
 Buddha
and we have much work in front of us.

Revel in your purity child.

for soon
you are going to let the whole world know of it.

The True Adventures of Jed Lightsear, Space Pirate!

By Ralph R. Raims

Illustrated by Bagwell

"Things might've been different if Gail, the pneumatic endorphin-spume dol, hadn't toppled past on her distractingly elegant pins ..."

ADVENTURES

OF

JED LIGHTSEAR,
SPACE PIRATE!

By Ralph R. Raims
Art by Bagwell

I

"Three Down at the Furt Fark Perimeter"

SHIT!

Things might've been different if Gail, the pneumatic endorphin-spume dol, hadn't toppled past on her distractingly elegant pins at precisely the moment Jed Lightsear chose to spatulate about access codes to the Furt Fark perimeter. (You remember Jed? Still talks a good sandwich, but you wouldn't trust him as far as you could spit him.) So there we are, me, Jed and Gail. Jed's like "it's amazing man..." some-such, and "two off the New Danube Delta - six back from Arcadia... yadda yadda" and I'm like "yeah yeah" 'cos Gail's pink nipples are winking at me over the top of her pink latex corset and her pink shiny lips are goin' "yeah, honey..."
(Down boy.)
Next thing you know we're high over mount Hubris watching the sparkles dancing out of Permafrost City like arc welding. I'm trying to concentrate on what Jed's saying, but Gail's got a four-digit handle on me and she's steering pretty good! Soon it's full nightscape and the wind is straightening even Jed's Dapper Dan hair as we take the "Taunton Excesses" down town to Port Miramax. (Yeah, old Jed always did have an eye for my ship. She's a babe, retro-styled custom scape-bender. Bit damned independent, but you gotta love her! Guess that's why he asked me along.)
And there it is. The Furt Fark perimeter. Bigger than Mohammed's mountain and twice as profound.
"Holy fucking Dick!" shouts Jed, laughing. It's some info-dump and no doubt! Our neuro-receptors are buzzing like 'Lectro-Wasps round a stat ball. Gail is spurting endorphins all over us, trying to fuck everything at the same time. I whip out the Exodus I acquired along Sunset B while I can still think clearly enough and drip 10ccs into our eyes. Soon we're flat out spin-drunk, talking Jungshit and passing round the "Blowman" tm, just like we used to in the Monde.
Then Gail's off, riding the monkey, and we can see the ectoplasmic trails drifting off her like spectral filigree.
"There she blows. Whoa yes." Jed, one eye half open, waves an arm in the general direction. "Listen, man. We got the codes. What say we check it out, you and me?"
"Jed Jed Jed." (I'm at the upper end and flying.) "I can't leave Gail. I'm hooked man. Proper bitten."
"Shit."
(You ever ride the monkey? One time you're down like a gump-child, all

Jungshitted out and dumbass. Next Spyro the giant cosmic monkey has manifested between your legs. Soon you're clinging on to that bright golden fur and bounding along the seventeenth dimension like it was a high wire, praying that the metawhals don't blunder into your plasma-trail and send you Crazyeddy.)

I can see Gail up ahead. Jed's whooping behind me. We ride the monkey all the way to Proto China Town.

The Aurora Hendrix is advertising Base Adaptoids when we come down. Below it the Synthtown New Bizley flashes smooth invites at us and, too down-dumb to argue, we climb back into the "Taunton Excesses" and let her take us in.

The Hyatt Flotel has sub-stratos rooms available so we take one.

Later, all honeyed up in the jack-ouzi, we plan our entry into the perimeter.

"I'll press the guardians with code - got it from an old acquaintance who broke into the Furt Fark half a lifetime back. Shit, the old freebootin' hobo's almost a god now, but he can still speak human enough - if you're patient." Jed says. "Gail, you gonna stick out honey, so spray 'em good. Keep 'em sweet."

We wake and dress in the splintered morning light, chopped and diced by the prismic windows of the Hyatt Flotel. Bathed in magenta, Gail smiles her fuckme smile then looks out at the perimeter. Jed, in cyan, slicks shut his suit. His smile cries "come on now baby dol. Come on baby." The suits make us look like highflights, cool and rich. We hide our smiles with trendy flute-masks. The air is cleaned and jacked up with nutrients. Our voices ring with harmonics. Mandelbrot shades hide our eyes behind a dancing spectrum, like diesel films over water.

"Come on now baby dol."

Later we ride the elevator shuttle back down to Bizley Town and take a rickshaw to the perimeter. The driver, a Spumoid, tries to charge us triple fare. He trembles, indignant - like a giant purple jellyfish - three feet above the ground, and finally stings us for double.

"Fucking highflights", he warbles.

"Fuck you!" Jed yells back. (Old Jed don't much like it when somebody gets one over on him. No sir.)

But we're at the perimeter.

(Remember the imagiplants we used to watch as kids? Sailing round the virtual Furt Fark perimeter together, thinking "this is what it must be like..."

It's not.

The effect the actual Furt Fark has on the body, even at distance, is near indescribable. Once, you'll recall, we gatecrashed the technotrance of 30,000,000 initiate Quantumonks and briefly glimpsed an abstraction of god - before they spotted us and drove us out of empathspace.

Not even close.

The Furt Fark takes you apart and puts you back together. Perfectly. It fills the quantum spaces between your atoms with a symphony of feathers cast from an angel's wings.)

Gail sprays and we're all like "Oh God oh God" and the Guardians - protected in their armor of rough-spun diamond punched into lead and shrouded in zappy plasmashields - ask for the codes.

Maybe it WAS the endorphins that got to him, though the flute-masks should have taken care of that. Maybe he lost it 'cos there was three of us there. Maybe the proximity of the Furt Fark made a better man of him and he couldn't lie. Or

"...too down-dumb to argue, we climb back into the *"Taunton Excesses"* and let her take us in. ."

maybe Jed pulled a fast one and worked those codes like they was basic trig. Whatever. Those Guardians soon had us rumbled good!
I unfolded the metascape access and jumped us three parsecs before they got off a single round.

12000 light-years away we booked into a lowpro sleep spa and zoned out for two weeks in zero-gravitanks.
Gail had been transfigured, I suppose. Her endorphin mists were laced with pheromones, and she had taken on a more organic shell. I'm pretty sure she was actually *alive* after that. Either way, somehow I wasn't enough for her anymore. Maybe I never was. She didn't much talk, just smiled a distant smile, and soon she was gone. Still hurts.
And Jed? Jed just fucked off.
The 'Taunton Excesses' paid our bill at the Hyatt Flotel and headed out to the Pyramid Nebula without incident. I met her, as arranged, at the Mountain Momma Inn, southside of the planet West Virginia. She pretended she was sad to find me all alone, but the next day she had gone too. (And to think of all the love I lavished on her! Bitch!
And you know what? I just bet Jed Lightsear knows EXACTLY where to find her...)

SHIT!

Octavia Flume once wrote that "The Tachion Tract is the model for human consciousness." I'm still puzzling over what she meant when suddenly I'm back in Mean Time and everything is dirty again. I had forgotten my knees ache when I walk. It's a short distance from the check-out desk to my car, but it reminds me.

II

"The Fly Trap"

"New Derby was built by adventurous midlanders with no imagination."
Mitch Cathode scratched the stump of his left arm, checking the plug points for inflammation before sliding his prosthetic back on. The fat barman of the "Spit and Gate" continued his practiced patwah.
"Luck-rich wideboys they were. Unfolded through the metascape and decided to make their home here, on Planet Elvis. "The most earth-like rock" - they proclaimed - "in the universe!" But it was only ten years before the *grass* on Planet Elvis woke up..."
Mitch flexed synthetic fingers, tingling with the return of sensation. "The grass." he said. "Tell me about the grass."
The inhabitants of Planet Elvis had not guessed at it's carnivorous nature. Half the population was painfully devoured, another quarter scarred and maimed, before it was finally cut. The corporation that founded the planet fought a hopeless lawsuit, but the facts were clear enough: They had not adequately studied the *grass*. And 360,000 people had died.
"You know that it's protected now? Yup. New Manhattan is a zoo for grass! They've built plastiglass walkways all over it in time for the next feed. Almost half a million Sheep, cattle and Wendigo have been imported just for the damn grass to eat!"

Mitch felt the codes jump in his fingertips as he left the pub. He had made do without his arm for a week, slumming it in a lowpro sleep spa in the Pyramid Nebula while Jed Lightsear worked his magic. He didn't much care for the Jungshitting widester, all slick-suited and Dapper-Danned, but he was the best.

"Get you into the fucking Furt Fark those codes man!" he said. "Straight and no dice! Getting in's the sweet bit, but you gotta get out like goose shit - hear me? These code's 'll get you out quick."

"There's something else." said Mitch. "It feels..."

"Just like the real thing, huh slick? Only *better*?"

And, yes, the arm was *exactly* like the real thing. *Better*. And something crawled up out of it and jump-started parts of his brain hitherto redundant.

"Oh man, you's digging it! Yeah, like that huh?" Lightsear was ecstatic, brimful of selflove and enthusiasm. "Know this Pinocchio, see dude? An endorphin-spume dol that saw God's toenails and came alive! I was with her - right there at the edge of all possibilities, looking into the *Total*! And now I can make this stuff *live*! See, it's just a case of getting the materials to perceive us in a new light, you chasing? It has to learn that WE'RE alive, and the strings click round to a whole new dimension man - just like a revolving gate - and matter reconfigures itself, and BANG! We're in a dialog man! It's all there, all to be had at the Furt Fark. Telling you."

"Right."

Mitch Cathode wasn't much interested in the Furt Fark. He imagined it, not entirely inaccurately, as a kind of reverse black hole. A galactic anomaly that proved everything right and everything wrong at the same time. Now it was a deleterious tourist attraction, jealously policed by the "Guardians", enhanced and embittered descendants of the prospectors that had long-ago chanced upon it.

It was raining.

New Derby, built in the classic fusion style of nineteenth century earth Victorian/twenty-first century Harryan, was a squat red brick and concrete sprawl. It's population opted to live in terraced dwellings along narrow streets, turning the sound up on their archaic six-D hard-light generators to avoid hearing the neighbors squabbling. Mitch Cathode liked it.

Back at the Cloughy Hotel he punched in for three hours deepsleep and an Ubersound-Flush detox. He wanted a clear head for the next day.

***

And suddenly he's on an Aeroflume, six hundred decks up over the Borstal Channel, and he can see New Manhattan swallowing waves on the horizon.

And suddenly he's passing his one small bag through the metascan, smiling pointlessly at the immigration officers, while his arm works the codes.

And suddenly he's through. He's there. Ten years, almost to the day, of waiting and planning and waiting some more. Ten years since the grass stole away his children, his beloved wives, tearing them from his arms, tearing *off* his arm.

He's there.
Here.
Now.
It's nearly time.

Mitch Cathode watches the sheep, cattle and Wendigo graze upon the dozing terror below through the plastiglass walls of the walkway, and smiles.

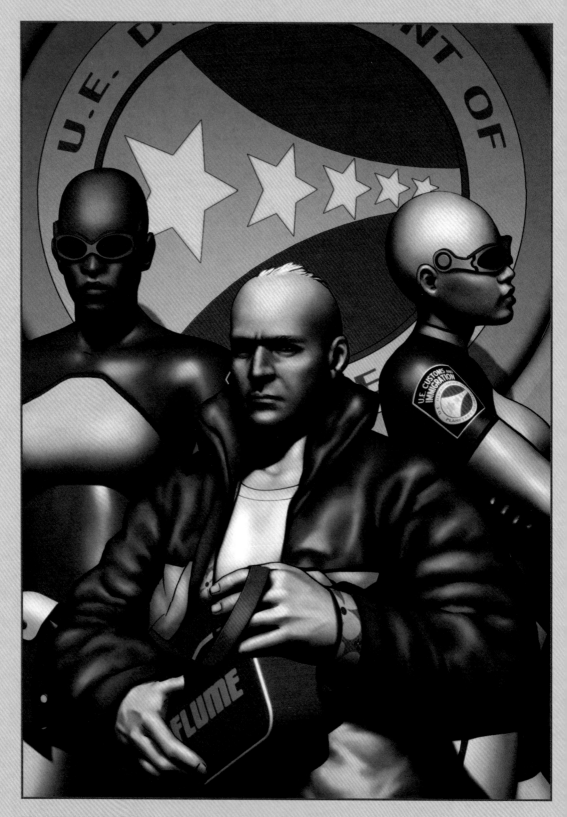

"And suddenly he's passing his one small bag through the metascan, smiling pointlessly at the immigration officers, while his arm works the codes. "

III

"Phoenix"

"D'you see that! Hoo Bo? D'you see what happened on New Manhattan man?"
Jed Lightsear was fully flow-moed, I mean slick was x-tatix!
"Check this Hoo Bo!" And boy he's thrusting the juddering Newsphere in my face,
all lit up with outerference - 'cos he's so scooped and won't stand still.
"Hey! Lube, dude!" I says. "Still youself boy! I can't see anything in this with you
all quiverin' like you a spumoid in a 'lectro-storm!"
I watched as the images settled, and there was New Manhattan - the grass zoo -
'cept below the plastiglass walkways that straddle the island the famous
carnivorous flora was all ablaze. The carcasses of it's once-to-be feast, imported
sheep and cattle from Earthside, Wendigo from Neoteric-Ukon, shuddered and
rippled like black and red jello in the heat waves.
"Uh huh." I says. "So. And what's got you all Hummin' Jack over this, slick? Did
another of your well-laids fuck up again?"
"Mitch Cathode man! He did it! And the codes worked man! Tellin' you, fell out
me pure and ripe and burnin'!"
And here I must have looked like the guy who blinked when Forman went down,
'cos I hadn't a whiff what flash-boy was spatulating about!
"Shit, Hoo Bo, for a Metragon" He's sayin' "You don't grock too good!"
Now us Metragons are empaths, not grockers, seers, sayers, readers or psychics.
All I knew was Jed was riding high on happy pheromones, and that was getting
me all messy and confused. I was starting to judder myself!
"Fuck, Jed! I don't know no Mitch Cathode! Slow down slick! Gimme the
pictures..."
So that's when he tells me about Mitch Cathode. Poor guy moved to Planet Elvis
just before the grass woke up. Lost his wives, six kids and an arm before he was
pulled to safety. Jed worked on a prosthetic for the guy, pumping it full of stolen
code when he was still coming down from his brush with the forces of creation
at the Furt Fark. And so it seems the guy had taken that code, busted through the
security at New Manhattan, and set the grass ablaze with six vials of Subatomic
Field Disrupters secreted in his new arm.
His revenge on the grass was complete.
Not only that, but Mitch Cathode wasn't even mentioned in the report. He'd
gotten away with it.
"Don't you see, Hoo Bo?" Says Jed, blue eyes child-bright and teeth flashing like
the moons of Po Nagarath rising over the frost-dunes of Ternne. "They WORKED!
The codes fucking worked, ya glean me?"

And that's all I know, 'cos Jed bein' Jed took off soon after that, and I never saw
the slick Jung-Shitter again but on Newspheres.
Anyhow, there you have it. The story of how Jed Lightsear cracked and tested the
stolen codes that unify matter, and headed out into the universe to see what he
could do with them...

IV

"Pirates of the Void"

"With an arch grin, Jed Lightsear waved at his would-be captors gathered at the fringe of the void-storm, unable to advance their pursuit.
"I'm afraid that Lady Luck as yet remains my bedfellow, my dear Major Todger!"
he said, and without further ado he swept Gail, the living endorphin-spume dol, up into his muscular arms and lithely sprang into the awaiting comforts of the "Taunton Excesses", his beloved ship ablaze with code and wonder.
"I'll get you yet Jed Lightsear!" yelled the Major into the sudden emptiness..."

***

"Muscular arms?" queried Gail. Jed grinned.
Mitch Cathode unlinked his prosthetic arm from the core of the ship's cortex becoming mostly just human again. "This Jed Lightsear seems like quite a guy. Like to meet him some day."
"Another bestseller complete! Gail, post it out for me baby, won't you? Usual channels. My fans will be missing me."
"The humility! No, really, Jed. It moves me." Jed watched Mitch shift his belligerent ruffled self out of the Nav-Hole. "I'm mush. Gonna slip me into some deepsleep, mayhaps get another ubersound-flush and detox this fucked old carcass."
"Hey baby, we ain't even partied yet!" Gail, pink and sleek, brushed his cheek with her sweet synthskin lips. "Don't poo-poo the rushes honey, we deserve what we got!"
"Not here for the laughs, dol, you know that. Just got nothin' else worth doing."
Jed laughed. "Sure are a fun-sponge mister! C'mon Gail, lets go fly with Spyro!" He disappeared below whistling "Honey Pie", brimful of his own id.
"Getting high ain't my thing, dol. Me? Sure, I like a drink. But I was just your regular Family Freddie, see? Nothing much special about me. Well - not back then anyhows...
"You go."
"OK honey pie, but only 'cos you told me. Gotta keep the great Space Pirate happy out here, otherwise he'll most probly drop me on some forgotten rock..."
Gail blew a sweet-scented pheromone-laced kiss at the older man and disappeared in Jed's wake.
Mitch Cathode sighed and removed the prosthetic limb that had changed him forever. It mewed at him, suffering a mild separation anxiety as he put it to one side. Mitch ignored it. Gently he scratched his stump, checking for any rashes or sores. There were none. He sighed and looked out of the viewscreen, seeing his face reflected there.
How in heaven's gate had he come to be here? Come to be a part of this gang, this ridiculous posse? Mitch Cathode, now one of the most wanted thieves in all known creation! Pirates of the void, and legends across the stars!
Perhaps, he mused, it *was* quite a tale after all...

"I'll get you yet Jed Lightsean!" yelled the Major into the sudden emptiness..."

V

Gail

Gail, the pneumatic endorphin-spume dol, found "life" to be a lucky-dip trip - and some. Her memories, her entire existence prior to the Furt Fark incident, were all intact - but detached, like memories of Spyro the Cosmic Monkey. Her hardwire still daddied large parts of her consciousness, she was an exotic sex toy, a plaything - one of billions created by an altruistic quintillionaire in the Uber-Fluxian Quadratic to ease the apathy that was bruising the sentient universe at the time. She could speak human behavior like a language, respond expertly to individual requirements, often requirements the individual did not know they possessed in any conscious way. She dug it. Men and women fell in love with her constantly, but back then she had possessed no *will* of her own. She would only *perform*. Now, well, it was different. Gail was starting to wake up to the fact that she had an incredible potential. Her circuitry could process information radically faster than her cohorts, even with their new Furt Farked enhancements. She was no longer governed by laws of robotics. She was a new form of uber-life with a great deal of power at her slender synthetic fingertips.

Gail was increasingly growing bored of Jed Lightsear, who's self-obssession had non-the-less been a conduit to genuine flat-faced wonder. The Furt Fark had awakened in him a metaphysical savant. It had opened a Potentiality Space in his otherwise in-turned mind, and there he fizzed, brim full of graceful solutions to many of the BIG questions regarding *matter* and *unity*. He found *code*. But nothing else had changed. He could no more learn from these innate skills than teach them. He had the safe crack to every bank vault in the universe, but he never saw that it was infact the key to *every single thing* in the universe. He had the power to unlock it all, but not the will - nor the intellect. And Gail was starting to realize exactly what true feelings were. She had luxed-up in Jed's company in her previous incarnation because he was such a tools-out hedonist. He was so in love with himself that she had found him a challenge. But newly eyes wide in the universe, she at first suffered strange nebulous pangs - which she later identified as loneliness - then began to see that of all the sentient life-forms in creation she had come across, Mitch Cathode had grown most similar to herself. While she had become more human, he was now partially machine. And they had both been touched by Furt Fark code in ways they had not fully realised, nor were they ever likely to. She was starting to develop needs. Behind the brash, elegant facade, a complex creature was emerging - full of questions, desires, hopes, wants and dreams. Mitch might be the only person who could ever truly understand her. She was falling in love with him. In love, for the first time in all the nine hundred and thirty seven S.E.Ys (Standard Earth Years) of her existence. And for the first time, though nobody would suspect it, she was facing a future where decisions would be made based as much on their emotional implications as on probability equations and math.

Octavia Flume wrote "The Three Laws of Sentience dictate that directional limpic-field input through a singularity at subatomic levels are the cause of common love."

"And that's when I twoc-ed my first ZX59, took it right out from under the slide-boy's receptors, and he didn't grock a thing. Yup. Me, I got the fingers, baby. I got the fucking fingers!" I was zero-graving in a swirl of purple Jubjub smoke living up the old times - nostalgia is Jubjub's shtick.

"Sure are slick, Jed." says Gail, but she was running auto-response - I could tell. See, she was out of the office and away making music with a devastated middle-aged man in her newly discovered imagination. That doll's wide awake now boy! Oh yes, eyes bright under the glare of the universe! And damned if she ain't falling for old Mitch, and I'm almost startin' to regret putting that code in his arm, 'cos space is a big empty place, and this man here has needs too, right? Yeah, you got me slick. I'm not so great about losing my relief valve to the fun-sponge.

Then: "THOOM!!" And there's a hole in the hull of The Taunton Excesses big enough to ride a Fnark through.

"What the fuck?" Me, pink-eyed, before all the air leaves the chamber and I'm going with it. Gail, moving like only she could, activates the Quantum Wall and throws me an airball.

"Stay here baby." she beams into my neuro-receptors, making me fuzzy and gump-child, despite the situation. "I'm going up front."

"Fuck it." I think. "Let the kids deal with it - and the Jubjub takes me back home for a while...

"Mamma, is that you? When's daddy coming home?"

Gail's   feeling   something   new   -
hermindmovesfastit'sthinkingfastandshedoesn'tknowshedoesn'tknowwhat/ifhe's/w
hatifhe'shurt?Whatthen?Hecan'tbe/Can'tbehurt/WhatthefuckWASthat?/she'sthinkin
g - and somewhere her logic centers wake up to the fact that she's scared, that she's actually afraid she might loose somebody.

"Gail, get up here. Need your speed toots."

And the squall in her circuits confuses her - just for a billisecond - then she smiles, and there's no process behind it. The first - the first! - completely spontaneous smile of her existence.

Mitch Cathode is OK.

"Looks like the Major found us. Any ideas how he might do that?"

Gail is in the seat beside Mitch, already plugging in. Another second and there's no need to talk. Mitch, Gail and The Taunton Excesses are one consciousness. The Quantum Wall takes a few more hits but holds, and soon they're half a galaxy away...

VI

Major Todger

"Fuck it! Fuck, damn and shit it! FUCK!"

"Sir? We've lost them again..."

I hate him. With every cell I loathe him. And what I can't understand, what really gnaws my balls, is that the fucker - with all the subtlety of a Harkassian Nargalope, and half the brain power - somehow plays me like Frankie Gump-fish!

"I can see that Private! Scan sectors 973X8 through 3566y9, and "The Flail". Use a Subatomic Pulse, then flash 'em a few Pinkies. That don't pick 'em up we'll call it a day. Fuck!"

My sweet aunt Tony used to say Jed Lightsear was a sainted sinner. Back then we used to cruise The Old Vendetta in our Stetson V-855, and all I saw was the spark in those zippy eyes, the dazzle of that smile. We did everything together, Jed and me. We paid for the V-855 by working Nemo's at the Weekout. Jed blagged a space in a grav block to store her, and we'd spend all our down time pampering the old lady. Boy was she ever pretty! Even Penny Cockslott, my high school sweetheart of four S.E.Ys, used to cotton to it when we pulled up in that baby - all retro cool and shimmering grav-reversers - blaring out old Neb Boy numbers from the vintage holopod.

I guess that's when things first turned bad. One Firstday Weekout I rolled up, as usual, to meet Jed and take the V-855 up The Chute for a blowout, only to find our block space empty. Jed, it turned out, had taken her cruising the Aurora Santiago - with Penny Cockslott! Seems he'd been slipping her the benefit of his no-doubt-about-it for months, and everybody knew, 'cept, of course, this gump-child. I'm much bigger than Lightsear, so I made sure he learned just how much. Got myself damn near kicked out of high school for that, my first ever transgression, but it was worth it.

True to form, Jed tired of Penny soon as it was yesterday's news. No good unless it's wrong, right? Left her bawling in my arms, wanting him so bad. I loved Penny Cockslott, and she loved Jed. Jed only loved one person in his life, and you don't need me to tell you who that was. Still, I forgave him, and damned if we weren't laughing it up on Iron-Side just a couple of months later.

(Never did forgive Penny though. Last I heard she married a Deep Space prospector and they vanished somewhere in the Darwin's Beard nebula.)

We was still best buddies two S.E.Ys later, until Jed - high as Ghobi's fruit sack on Coolak - broke into my father's townhouse in Thatcherville, threw a party, stole his favorite watch and painted "Rich Todger fucks fish" on the garage doors.

And somehow it's me that ends up at military academy.

Even so, on leave one time I bumped into Jed at the "Return of the Swing" in downtown Paluka, sipping Vurtbombs. Slick fucker's got a girl on each arm and his eyes are all aglow with flux-plants, so he's constantly getting distracted by people's visually enhanced auras. Before you know it we're heading into the Drop-Zone with Brendina and Pi, and Jed suggests we take a ride up to the Monde and book into a flotel, maybe pass round a "Blowman" tm. Jed liked it at the Monde - guess we all did back then - and he was it's self-styled king. Every Jungshitting widester there knew his tune and how to blow it.

What happens? Fucker dropped a Quaglug in my beer, sends me into the the metascape where I'm found by a pilgrimage of quantumonks who grock I'm a soldier - and you can see where that's going! - while he fucks Brendina and Pi in the zero-gravitank. When I'm finally back inside my head he's split, leaving me with the bill and no fucking eyebrows.

That fucking fucker! FUCK!!

I went out to the Tertial Pariah Belt after that. Lost an eye and some brain in the Thought Wars. Got enough medals to build a shuttle out of. And when I heard Jed Lightsear was wanted across the known universe for a series of crimes as foolhardy as they were audacious and remarkable, I knew I was the man to go after him.

Oh yes. I'll get you yet, Jed Lightsear...

To be continued...

NECROMACHIA

WORDS : LIAM SHARP

ART : LEE CARTER

NECROMACHIA!
That's what we call it. This place. This endless cavity of rotting machinery and wailing pipes.
Last night I remembered something. Something important. An image I saw as a child.
In it somebody had painted a ceiling bright blue. And a voice - our father? - was telling us not to forget.

For you see, the blue ceiling was itself a reminder. It represented a great concept. A philosophy.
The "OUTSIDE".
Do you recall it? How we would dream of such things back then?
How soon dreams fade here - where every door, every portal, leads to more of the same.

The hydroponics sustain us.
The air forever circulates.

We live, but hardly thrive.

Up here I found a *reason*.
The "Outside", the blue ceiling, and something else -
Something I read, once, that had been scrawled on a wall.
I wrote it down, but only recently did I understand it -
I pieced it all together, bit by bit.
And now I see HIM.

"And like a giant rolling automaton the Maker came to Necromachia and grew.
And if life there was, well then, it would be his.
The horror of space he would not abide,
nor the trappings of ownership,
the theft called possession.
He would fill it - everything! - with himself.
He would grow until there was no outside left to trap him, and nowhere to be lost.
He would take this outside and wrap himself around it."

I see you, Maker.
So great that you became lost even to yourself.
Lost *within* yourself.
And we, your children, are lost within you.
Unborn.

I hope you find it, up here, scrawled on another neglected wall in another neglected chamber.
Don't follow me down - down amongst the billion ghosts of Necromachia - where I seek freedom.
But only *remember,* and go *looking...*

But somewhere - just around the corner - just below our feet - in the room next-door - the ceiling is *blue*.
And you can fly up through it, and just keep going.

There the air is like cold water on a hot face.
And there are people -
I can almost hear them laughing.

Look beyond the bars and you'll see light.
Not the unforgiving orange that drops our eyes into pitch pools and makes skulls of our faces
Nor the indifferent electric blue that bleaches and flattens everything until it loses all form and purpose...

But a golden warm light that no God could ever trap.

Mam Tor Pin-up Gallery

Necromachia

By Brem

STEVE
PERKINS

Regular Edition:
"Herycel Ben Egan
outside the gates
of 'Tantrix Alumnae'
By Liam Sharp

Enhanced Edition:
Untitled

By Glenn Fabry

STORY, SUCH AS IT IS, AND ART BY KEV CROSSLEY